Madame VO

Madame VO

Vietnamese Home Cooking
FROM THE
New York Restaurant

Photography by
ANDREW BUI

JIMMY LY & YEN VO
with DAN Q. DAO

ABRAMS,
NEW YORK

CONTENTS

Chapter I:

From Vietnam to New York
Pickles, Sauces, and Condiments

Chapter V:

Our Past, Present, and Future
Desserts and Drinks

The Madame Vo Mini-Guides

Introduction

Do It for
the Culture

For many years, word on the street was that
you could find any cuisine in New York
City—*besides* Vietnamese. Despite its rep-
utation as one of the world's food capitals, the city
was long described as a "Vietnamese food desert,"
with the exception of some old-guard phở shops
in Chinatown. But change was in the air in 2017,
around the time my wife, Yen Vo (that's *Madame
Vo* to you), and I opened our first restaurant in
Manhattan despite no business plan, no PR, no
connections—just blind faith in our real homestyle
Vietnamese cooking and the food we grew up with.

That's the food you'll find in this cookbook, which
shares a collection of recipes that define the ethos
of Madame Vo, the restaurant we opened seven
years ago on a tree-lined block of East Tenth Street.
Some are dishes we've served to thousands of
guests, like the flagship Madame Phở (page 129),
our take on Vietnam's national noodle soup dish.
Others are dishes we grew up with, homestyle family meals that our busy parents would whip up on
weeknights, like Spring Rolls (page 84) and fried

rice (pages 148–49). Then there are the dishes that
transport us to our travels in Vietnam, including a
Beef in Betel Leaf recipe (page 95) that we teased
out of a street vendor in Ho Chi Minh City (colloqui-
ally referred to as Saigon).

A few more are original recipes that were inspired
by childhood memories—including trips I took with
my parents to Little Saigon in California—and there
are recipes that are deeply personal to us, like the
pandan honeycomb cake (page 214) that Yen and
her mom would make together during her mom's
tough battle with cancer. All these dishes mean
something to us, our families, and our loyal diners.
Now, we're sharing them all with you.

As we look back to the day we opened Madame
Vo's doors, we can't forget that we had no idea
whether it would work out. In fact, for a while at the
very beginning, it really looked like it wasn't going
to (you'll have to read the rest of the book for the
full story). We didn't even know what month or day
would be best to open the restaurant (they say it's

best to open right before peak dining seasons such as the fall). There was zero strategy. We truly just winged it and opened our doors in January 2017.

As you've probably surmised, things eventually shook out in our favor—thanks to a little bit of New York magic and a whole lot of hard work. Since opening, our humble restaurant has been blessed with regulars from our East Village neighborhood as well as visitors from every corner of the world— from the East Coast to East Asia. We feel incredibly lucky to have been able to share Vietnamese food with the thousands of guests who've come through our doors—from our friends and family to actors, designers, and famous chefs we thought we'd only ever see on TV.

Throughout the years, we've weathered the normal ups and downs of running a small restaurant and overcome the fallout of a global pandemic that unfortunately shuttered our second concept, Madame Vo BBQ, which at the time was the first-ever Vietnamese restaurant to be reviewed by *New York Times* critic Pete Wells. (Don't worry, we've since turned that space into Madame Vo's brother restaurant, Monsieur Vo.) But it wasn't until we started writing this book that we took the time to look back at this journey in its entirety and reflect on the lessons we've learned.

What does this mean for you at home? Thanks to Vietnamese chefs, restaurateurs, and food entrepreneurs, Vietnamese food is more accessible than ever before. These days, fish sauce can be found in almost any supermarket, and thanks to the internet, you don't need a cookbook to find some basic recipes for Vietnamese food. That said, we believe people are eager to delve deeper into Vietnamese cooking and would appreciate our guidance on getting started, and how to take classic dishes to the next level. We hope you'll feel the love and care we poured into putting together these recipes so they are easy to follow, no matter your experience level. We think these are the best Vietnamese recipes out there, especially the ones that have been passed down to us from family members.

After all, each recipe in this cookbook-memoir is a story that recounts the moments we've celebrated as well as the blood, sweat, and tears we've shed along the way in our process of creating Madame Vo. And this book is a way to honor our parents, from whom we got our recipes, and a way to share our journey with our two sons, who we hope will learn from our experiences and take pride in what our family has accomplished.

In fact, family is a central theme of this cookbook. Many of the featured dishes are direct transcriptions of recipes from my family and Yen's, while others are adaptations or hybrids of recipes from both sides of the family. For me, food and family are synonymous. I learned how to cook at home, from my parents, who both had experience in the restaurant industry. I'm not a classically trained chef. I never went to culinary school. But I was my family's sous chef. Hosting big parties is typical for Vietnamese families, and food is always the main event. So, from the time I was a child, my dad taught me how to pick fruit at a supermarket and how to hold a

knife, and I would help my mom chop herbs and prep meats.

But our parents gave us more than just recipes, knowledge of ingredients, and skills in the kitchen. They also taught us the value of hard work. Like many first-generation Asian Americans, I grew up caught between two worlds—the world of my parents, who fled a war-torn country as refugees, and my world: America, New York City, Queens. As a kid, I sometimes resented them for working long hours; as an adult, I wanted to earn their respect. But ultimately, I'm grateful to them and the sacrifices they've made. I credit them with my work ethic and scrappiness.

To build on the foundation our parents had laid, Yen and I adopted a motto that has guided us since day one: "Do it for the culture." And that includes my mom's Vietnamese culture, my father's Teochew Chinese culture (for more on this, see page 73), and the New York City culture that we live and breathe. In Asian culture, where so much remains

unspoken, food is oftentimes how we express ourselves and our love for one another. This is true for both me and Yen, who shares similar memories with her own family.

When Yen and I met, the first thing we bonded over was food. On one of our earliest dates, I took her home to my family in Queens for a taste of my mom's homestyle cooking. From our early courtship days, Yen and I built our relationship on our shared love for food, our culture, and our families. I taught her about Malaysian food from Queens; she taught me about Creole food from the Gulf Coast. And Madame Vo's menu is a testament to our upbringings: the double-fried, fish sauce–glazed wings (page 74) are a Super Bowl Sunday recipe from Yen's dad, Anh Vo, while the tomato-accented fried rice (page 148) is one of my favorite things that my mom makes.

So, as you read this book, we hope you'll see that Madame Vo is a symbol of perseverance, triumph, and love between me and my wife, Yen. The Madame

Vo story is an only-in-NYC tale about a restaurant kid from Queens who couldn't see himself do anything else in life besides cooking and sharing Vietnamese culture with the world. We hope these recipes bring as much joy to you and your family as they have for many generations of ours.

HAPPY COOKING!

**CHEF JIMMY LY, YEN VO,
and the Madame Vo team**

Grandparents and the kids visiting us at work on the weekends

FROM VIETNAM TO NEW YORK

A Love Letter to Vietnamese Refugees

My story began when my parents decided to leave everything they knew and go to a completely foreign country. I share a similar background with my wife, Yen: Her family is from Rạch Giá in southwestern Vietnam, but she was born in a refugee camp in Thailand. After being sponsored by a church to come to Michigan in April 1986, her family relocated two years later to Mississippi, where her father, Anh Vo, found work as a fisherman. To tell the story of Vietnamese food in America is to tell the modern history of Vietnam and its diaspora.

To be honest, our parents are our heroes, and if it weren't for their bravery—a sacrifice shared by hundreds of thousands of Southeast Asian refugees—none of us would be here today. Yen and I do what we do to show them our appreciation and love.

My mom, Phung Kim Cuc, was born in Mỹ Tho, a southern city in the Mekong Delta region of Vietnam. After moving to Saigon during the preamble to the Vietnam War, she sold smoothies to make a living. She wasn't wealthy, but she made do.

By contrast, my father, Kieng Ly, who is of Cambodian and Chinese (Teochew, specifically) descent, was born in Cambodia to a well-to-do family that owned factories producing textiles and ice cream. In 1970, he fled to Saigon (now Ho Chi Minh City) to escape the violent genocide by the Khmer Rouge, during which his family lost everything they owned, and many family members and friends went missing. After moving to Vietnam, my dad learned Vietnamese, which he still speaks today, in addition to Khmer, Teochew, and Cantonese (though we all identify predominantly as Vietnamese).

Nearly fifty years ago, in April 1975, South Vietnam fell to North Vietnam. In the years that followed, Vietnam suffered greatly both economically and politically, spurring a mass exodus of refugees, and many former South Vietnamese soldiers who couldn't escape were sent to re-education camps by the newly unified Communist government. And though the United States had withdrawn from their conflict, war in Vietnam was far from over. As American soldiers returned to their wives and children, Vietnamese soldiers would fight a series of "forgotten wars" in 1978, with Cambodia, and in 1989, with China.

LEFT TO RIGHT:
Dad tried his best to take me out on his days off.

My parents in the streets of Chinatown, New York

Dad, young and determined, arrived to New York City with big hopes and dreams.

Yen with her parents in New Orleans

During this time of chaos, my dad sold cigarettes (often counterfeit versions) in Saigon to get by. It was just enough to help take care of his family. My mom likewise was continuing to run her smoothie stand. But it would be years before they'd meet. In response to increased uncertainty, my mother's family fled by boat—risking the possibility of death by drowning, dysentery, or pirate raids. According to the United Nations High Commission for Refugees, it's believed that anywhere from two hundred thousand to four hundred thousand Vietnamese and Southeast Asian people lost their lives at sea. Luckily, my mother's boat was picked up by an American ship in 1981, which took them to a refugee camp in the Philippines.

My father escaped first to Thailand in 1980, then Indonesia, where he lived in a refugee camp and learned English. After five years, he received the necessary paperwork to seek asylum in the United States with a sponsorship from the Catholic church. His first stop was Philadelphia, Pennsylvania, where he lived in a shelter, wearing donated clothes and receiving a ten-dollar allowance each week, and took odd jobs: washing

dishes, carrying supplies, and working with a moving company.

Two months later, my dad made the fateful decision to board a bus to New York City, having heard of a growing Vietnamese Chinese community in Chinatown. He ended up at a small residential building at 221 Henry Street, where he knocked on the wrong apartment and fell in love instantly with the woman who opened the door. As it turns out, my mom had also found her way to Chinatown, where she was living in a three-bedroom apartment with eight other people. As she tells us, my father kept coming back, bringing flowers each time in an effort to woo her. And fast-forward a few years to 1985, I was born—an only child.

Though my parents' journey to the US is remarkable, it's one among millions—nearly eight hundred thousand Vietnamese refugees came to America between 1975 and 1985. And that's not to mention those who landed in Canada, Australia, Europe, and beyond. This book is a tribute to all those who crossed oceans, fled persecution, and risked their lives to give their children a chance at a better future.

On Vietnamese Culinary Philosophy and History

At Madame Vo, we find a balance between traditional—many of our dishes are prepared as they have been for generations in our families—and modern, in that we use higher-quality ingredients with an emphasis on service and presentation that's informed by my experience as a New York City diner. To make the most of this cookbook, it's worth getting to know some of the cultural principles and geographic factors that have shaped Vietnamese food throughout history.

Perhaps some of the most defining traits of Vietnamese food are colonialism, resilience, and adaptation. Before the era of French colonialism in the nineteenth century, Vietnam spent a millennium resisting, succumbing to, and rebelling against the Chinese to the north. It is believed that Vietnam was under some form of Chinese rule—with rebellions interspersed throughout—between 111 BCE and 938 CE. Some forty percent of the Vietnamese language uses words borrowed from Chinese.

This same phenomenon occurs in food. Vietnamese dishes not only employ many traditionally Chinese ingredients—rice noodles, braises, soy sauce—but the cuisine is shaped by aspects of a Buddhist-influenced philosophy, which teaches that food is not just meant for nourishment and pleasure, but also for health. Every ingredient used is intentional.

Framed in the context of Wu Xing, the concept of five elements central to traditional Chinese philosophy, the Vietnamese palate emphasizes a balance of the five basic tastes: salty, sweet, sour, bitter, and spicy. Each of these corresponds to an element of nature, each of which in turn is related to a bodily organ and a color (more of a general energy than a literal color). These foundational principles are not strictly followed today. In practice, all you need to know is that there are ancient, existential reasons why Vietnamese cooking emphasizes a very equitable balance of flavors in every meal.

Aside from a harmony of tastes, colors, and elements, Vietnamese food also relies on complementary and contrasting textures: a complete Vietnamese meal will often include ingredients that are soft and chewy, like noodles, along with crunchy, fried toppings and crisp, fresh herbs. The frequent use of dipping sauces and other condiments adds further depth, allowing diners to create different flavor and texture combinations throughout the course of a meal.

TASTE	ELEMENT	ORGAN	COLOR
Salty	Water	Bladder	Black
Sweet	Earth	Stomach	Yellow
Sour	Wood	Gallbladder	Green
Bitter	Fire	SM Intestine	Red
Spicy	Metal	LG Intestine	White

LEFT: baby snails (ốc ruốc) RIGHT: lemongrass and yellow onions

Vietnamese food, especially when fried, is often intended to be eaten with your hands—by wrapping lettuce around the fried bite along with other vegetables and herbs, and then dipping the wrap into a sauce, and engaging all your senses.

The cooking of Vietnam strays from Chinese influence largely in this obsession with fresh ingredients. Because of Vietnam's generally warmer, tropical Southeast Asian climate, it's abundant in peppers, spices, tropical fruit, and herbs—like lemongrass, mint, and cilantro. Vietnam's more than two thousand miles of coastline also yields an abundance of fresh seafood, with dishes like sea snails becoming national staples. Meanwhile, its more temperate highland regions produce historically Western ingredients like coffee and strawberries.

Vietnam's unique location—at a proverbial corner of mainland Southeast Asia—has also meant a long history of trading with the Indian subcontinent, whose cuisine has influenced every country in the region. Ports like ancient Hoi An were vital stops in maritime Southeast Asian trading routes, inviting the trade of Indian spices like cardamom and turmeric. Our Vietnamese Chicken Curry (page 111) is an example of this cultural exchange.

Chinese and Indian influences are present in the cuisine of Vietnam and its western neighbors, Laos and Cambodia, which together formed the entire colony of French Indochina. The French had established trading posts in Vietnam as early as the 1600s, though the official colonial period was only six decades long, ending in 1954.

French colonialism was a period of violence, discrimination, and hunger in the region, but it yielded some interesting cultural byproducts. In addition to Catholicism and a Romanized alphabet, the French also brought with them foods like coffee (café in French, cà phê in Vietnamese) and cheese (fromage in French, phô mai in Vietnamese).

Then there was, of course, the baguette, French bread that Vietnamese cooks have since adapted—Vietnamese bread typically has a softer exterior than its French counterpart, with an airier and lighter inside—and used to create the beloved, ubiquitous bánh mì. Vietnam's take on a sandwich is typically made with various cold cuts, pâté, fresh mayo, pickled carrots and daikon, cilantro, jalapeños, and more (see pages 122, 124, and 127).

The French used food as a weapon to assert their dominance over their colonial subjects. During French rule, only Westerners had access to French food—and they were also discouraged from eating local cuisine. Bread, in particular, was seen as superior to rice. Because wheat doesn't grow well in tropical climates, it was all imported and therefore unattainable for the average Vietnamese person. "Bread and meat make us strong, rice and fish keep them weak" was conventional French wisdom of the era.

It wasn't until World War I, when the French seized German import companies in Southeast Asia, that Western foodstuff would become available at discounted prices. Condensed milk would be fused with local coffee, and Maggi—the Swiss sauce we use in this book—became a preferred seasoning. Vietnamese people—both in Vietnam and the thousands sent to fight in Europe on behalf of the French—soon developed a taste for these new ingredients.

So, while the French introduced certain foods to Vietnam, and typically refused to eat any local dishes, it was Vietnamese cooks, operating with ingenuity in the face of great adversity, who turned mundane ingredients into the vibrant, flavorful food we love today.

All in all, Vietnam as we know it today has only existed since the mid-twentieth century. Even our national dish, the rice noodle soup phở, is not yet two hundred years old. Some say the dish emerged from Chinese noodle hawkers in the north, who brought rice noodles to Vietnam, while others say it takes its name from the French beef stew known as pot-au-feu (phở when pronounced correctly as "fuh" sounds a bit like "feu"). But whatever its precise origins may be, phở is not an ancient dish.

And Vietnamese food, while rich in tradition, is dynamic and ever evolving. So, whenever people claim to know exactly where a Vietnamese dish comes from, take it with a grain of salt. We believe that we shouldn't hesitate to continue to evolve the cuisine, based on our own local ingredients and traditions.

Bàn Cờ Market in District 3, Saigon

The Vietnamese Kitchen and Pantry

TOOLS: There are a few tools that you'll need to cook through this book–luckily, you'll probably have most on hand already, and the rest should be inexpensive to acquire. The gear we have compiled below are all workhorses that you'll be grateful to have on hand, from large stockpots for broths to the trusty Chinese cleaver, which is a favorite in Asian kitchens for a reason.

Butcher's Knife
As the name implies, these heavy-duty knives are designed to break down large pieces of meat. They typically come 6 to 8 inches (15 to 20 cm) long with a broad blade that curves up at the tip. The size of the blade helps with consistent slicing on large cuts of meat, while the thickness of the knife helps it to cut through bones and tough pieces of meat.

Cheesecloth
Cheesecloth is a loose, breathable cotton fabric used in the kitchen for straining. In this book, we use cheesecloth for straining spices from stocks as well as making desserts: Notably, we use cheesecloth to make pandan extract from scratch for our Pandan Waffles (page 221).

Chinese Cleaver
One of the most essential tools in an Asian kitchen, a Chinese cleaver is thinner than your usual butcher's knife, but much larger than a small paring blade. This makes it an extremely versatile general-purpose kitchen knife that can chop, slice, mince, and crush many ingredients. We use our cleaver for precise dicing and slicing of vegetables and boneless cuts of meat.

Do not use the cleaver to hack at bone or it will dull rapidly (for that, use the much thicker and heavier butcher's knife, see left). Funny story: When I first bought my dad a super-pricey chef's knife, he told me, "This doesn't have shit on my thirty-dollar cleaver!"

Clay Pot
Vietnamese clay pots are ideal for slow simmered and stewed dishes. The porous clay used to make them helps regulate heat and ensure even cooking. In this book, we don't use them for cooking, but you may use them for serving dishes like the Caramelized Fish (page 179) and the Caramelized Pork Belly with Egg (page 175), as they are useful for keeping dishes warm and are an attractive way to showcase traditional Vietnamese cookware.

Ladle
A ladle is a deep spoon that can be used to serve soups, gravies, and sauces. We recommend using a ladle for all our soup dishes, as well as for saucier noodles, like our Seafood Crispy Noodles with Gravy (page 144), which are covered in a thick, gravy-like sauce.

Large Stockpot
You'll need a large, deep pot (at least 8 quarts or liters, preferably 12) for making broths and stocks that are simmered evenly for long periods of time. As some dishes are highly labor-intensive to make, Vietnamese people tend to cook for the entire family, making complicated stocks in larger batches and freezing the leftovers. Having a big pot will save you time in the long run.

Mandoline
A mandoline is a slicing tool that is used to cut vegetables and fruits into uniform sizes. Adjusting the blade will yield slices based on your desired thickness. A mandoline comes in handy when making our Pickled Vegetables (page 45), an important condiment for many Vietnamese dishes.

Mortar and Pestle
A mortar and pestle is a two-part device generally made from ceramic or stone. The mortar is the bowl, and the pestle is a blunt handheld stick used to crush and grind ingredients like spices, garlic, and chiles into a fine paste or powder. You'll need to use a mortar and pestle for our Vietnamese Dipping Sauce (page 46), to smash up the Thai chiles.

Nonstick Frying Pan

The first cooking tool I ever learned to use was a nonstick skillet—a flat-bottomed pan that can be used for searing, frying, and browning food.

Noodle Strainer Basket

Asian noodle strainers are typically deep wire baskets with long wooden handles. These are, of course, great for when you are removing noodles from boiling water, but they also will come in handy for washing and blanching vegetables. To use the noodle strainer basket, you can put the uncooked noodles inside and dunk it into boiling water. Being able to quickly submerge and remove the noodles is especially handy for phở (pages 123, 129, and 132) since rice noodles cook fast.

Rice Cooker

This device can be found in almost any Asian kitchen and is designed to cook a variety of rice and grains. Because modern, electric rice cookers are automatic and deliver consistent results, they free us up to work on other tasks while the rice is being made. Choose a model with a nonstick bowl, automatic shut-off, and a large cooking capacity of at least 5 cups (1.2 liters). Rice cooker capacities always refer to uncooked rice. Our personal favorite is a Japanese rice cooker, Zojirushi, as it is durable and customizable.

Saibashi (Large Cooking Chopsticks)

Commonly made from bamboo or wood, these cooking chopsticks can be 13 to 18 inches (33 to 45 cm) long. I always use these to keep my hands away from the heat when cooking, to stir ingredients, or extract things from jars. When serving meals or removing something from hot oil, these can also be used as tongs. I prefer these to tongs as you have more control. When extracting something that is being fried, they don't pick up as much residual oil as tongs.

Saucepan

A saucepan is a deep stovetop pan with a long handle and a lid. Deeper than a standard frying pan but shallower than a stockpot, it is best for cooking liquid and can also be used for frying. Saucepans are made from materials like stainless steel, copper, aluminum, and enamel-coated metal. Because of the number of sauces we make, it will be necessary. You will use the saucepan with both savory recipes, like when you are frying potatoes for our Chicken Curry (page 111), and sweet dishes, like when you are making the coconut sauce for our Tricolor Dessert (page 210).

Steamer Basket

Perforated with small holes, these baskets are designed to be placed inside a covered pot and hold foods (like vegetables or dumplings) over simmering water to cook. Though some are made of bamboo, we use the stainless-steel variety in our kitchen. In this cookbook, a steamer basket will be needed for dishes like our Bánh Bột Chiên (page 85) and Bánh Chuối Hấp (page 217).

Wok

Woks are round-bottomed cooking vessels with high sides. Ubiquitous and essential in Asian kitchens, they are primarily used for stir-frying, or fast sautéing, without the need for lots of oil. The round bottom of a wok concentrates the heat, and the high sides retain it, more so than in a skillet or frying pan, so your food can cook in less time. The ideal tool for making stir-fries, woks can also be used to deep-fry or steam if you have a steamer basket.

When choosing a wok, I prefer cast-iron or blue carbon steel. A nonstick stainless steel wok isn't truly a wok because, even though it's the same shape, it won't heat food the same way. Beginner cooks can always use these to get used to the shape, though, no problem. Steel woks come with a dark glaze and are sometimes coated in oil. To "season a wok," or prepare a wok for its first-time use, heat it on the stovetop and burn off all the oil. The color may change, and the oil film will burn off, creating some smoke. Then, remove it from the heat, let it cool down, and brush it with fresh cooking oil. To clean the wok after cooking, do not wash it for too long or use harsh chemicals as this will strip off the seasoning—just a little water and soap will do.

Repeated use and seasoning of the wok will allow you to achieve what we call "wok hei" or the "wok breath"—referring to the signature smoke, seasoning, and flavor that is created when you use the wok regularly at high heat.

SPICES: The Vietnamese spice cabinet is relatively simple, as many everyday dishes are seasoned primarily with sauces, namely fish sauce, as well as pastes, like shrimp paste. Half of the spices in this list are used primarily just for Vietnam's national dish, the noodle soup phở (pages 123, 129, and 132), to which they're essential. Most can be found in supermarkets but are also easily ordered online.

Black Pepper / Tiêu Đen
Black pepper is essential to Vietnamese cuisine, and has always been, as it is grown throughout Vietnam from the Central Highlands to the resort island Phú Quốc. We pride ourselves on having some of the world's best black pepper, so it makes sense that it's used in just about every kind of Vietnamese dish (see the note).

Cardamom / Thảo Quả
Cardamom is an aromatic spice used in both savory and sweet Vietnamese dishes, most notably phở. Grown primarily in the Central Highlands, its presence speaks to the global influences on Vietnamese cuisine, including Chinese and Indian.

Cinnamon / Cây Quế
Cinnamon is another warming aromatic spice that finds its way into the stock for Vietnam's national dish, phở (pages 123, 129, and 132), along with Vietnamese spiced beef stew, or Bò Kho (page 109). In dishes like this, it's often combined with cardamom and star anise. Like cardamom, star anise, and coriander seeds, it'll be toasted for maximum flavor before it's added to the stock.

Coriander Seeds / Hạt Ngò
Though Mediterranean in origin, coriander seeds are used widely in Vietnamese dishes. In this book, you'll use them for both versions of our phở (pages 123, 129, and 132). We toast the seeds to draw out the warm, earthy, and peppery notes, which are crucial for the stock.

Curry Powder / Bột Cà Ri
While Vietnam is not as known for curries as countries like India, Malaysia, and Thailand, Vietnamese cuisine does boast one major standout take on Chicken Curry (page 111), which is the main reason you'll need to get your hands on some curry powder.

Fennel Seed / Hạt Tiêu Mèo
Fennel seed is widely used in Vietnamese cooking, particularly in dishes with meat, chicken, and seafood, like our Sour Soup with Shrimp (page 107). It offers a licorice-like quality.

Five-Spice Powder / Ngũ Vị Hương
Five-spice powder is a blend of cinnamon, fennel seeds, cloves, star anise, and Szechuan peppercorns. It's used widely in Chinese-influenced dishes like roast pork and roast duck. You'll also find it in our savory beef stew Bò Kho (page 109).

Rock Sugar / Đường Phèn
Rock sugar is a form of unrefined sugar that adds a more subtle sweetness and honeyed flavor. It's noted for its use in phở (pages 123, 129, and 132).

Star Anise / Quả Hồi
Star anise is an essential aromatic spice that's often described as having a sweet, licorice-like taste. It's often toasted, alongside cinnamon, cardamom, star anise, and fennel seed, then added to stocks and braises. Star anise is emblematic of the Vietnamese palate as it appears across soups, grilled meats, desserts, and drinks.

A NOTE ON PEPPER
White pepper and black pepper come from the same plant, *Piper nigrum*, but they are processed differently, which gives them different flavors and aromas. While black pepper is made from dried unripe berries that are briefly fermented, white pepper is made from ripe berries that have had the outer layer removed. The former has that signature bold, earthy taste of pepper, and the latter is milder. We use white pepper in recipes where we still want the peppery undertone but dialed down.

CLOCKWISE FROM TOP LEFT: rock sugar, cardamom pods, fennel seeds, star anise, coriander seeds, and cinnamon

PANTRY INGREDIENTS: Vietnamese cooking relies on a variety of seasoning sauces and pastes of both Vietnamese and Chinese origin. So, if you don't usually make Asian food at home, you may have to purchase some ingredients (but you'll be able to use them across multiple recipes). To help you decipher the plethora of online options, we've listed the key sauces we use—along with the brands we prefer, when applicable.

Chicken Bouillon

Chicken bouillon is made from dehydrated chicken stock, dehydrated vegetables, fat, and salt. It also often includes seasonings such as coriander, parsley, turmeric, and in many cases, MSG. Bouillon is most commonly found in the form of dry cubes of packed powder but is also available in a loose powder or paste form. You're welcome to use your preferred chicken bouillon, but we tend to call for measurements by the spoonful, so a powder like Totole Granulated Chicken Soup Base Mix may be easiest. Store in a cool, dry place such as a pantry for up to one year after opening.

Crab Paste

Subtly briny and rich, crab paste is created by cooking ground crabs with oil and spices. Not to be confused with crab fat, which is a mixture of fresh crab roe and innards also common in Southeast Asian cooking, crab paste is a flavorful shelf-stable seasoning that comes in handy when basting proteins as they cook, as well as in soup bases and fried rice. Generally, the brighter the paste, the better the quality. We use the brand Por Kwan. Store in the refrigerator for up to three months after opening.

Fish Sauce

Fish sauce is the mother sauce of Vietnamese cooking, lending a multi-layered umami flavor into hundreds of Vietnamese dishes and dipping sauces. Originally produced in southern Vietnam (and described in literature as the grand cru of Phu Quoc Island), it's derived from pressing, salting, and fermenting anchovies. There are many brands making fish sauce, but at our house, we prefer the Viet Huong brand, which features three crabs on the label. It's not too sweet or salty, hitting the right balance for our dishes. Store in a cool, dry place such as a pantry for up to a year after opening.

Golden Mountain Seasoning Sauce

Also popular in Thai cooking, this seasoning sauce is made of soybeans, salt, and wheat flour. It's often compared to both soy sauce, which is also made with fermented soybeans, and Maggi Seasoning Sauce, a vegetable-based concentrate, but is both saltier and sweeter. A little bit goes a long way in dishes like our Caramelized Fish (page 179) and in the dressing for our Papaya Salad (page 99). Store in a cool, dry place such as a pantry for up to a year after opening.

Hoisin Sauce

Another condiment used primarily in Vietnamese cuisine for phở, hoisin sauce is a sweet sauce made with fermented soybean paste, garlic, vinegar, and sugar. It has a thick ketchup-like consistency. Recommended brands include Lee Kum Kee and, our personal favorite, Koon Chun. Store in the refrigerator for up to a year after opening.

Huy Fong Chili Garlic Sauce

Made of ground chiles, garlic, and vinegar, this bright red Asian chili sauce is made of a similar set of ingredients as the familiar Sriracha condiment, also made by Huy Fong, but has a runnier texture and packs more direct heat and garlic flavor. We use it to season dishes like our Lemongrass Beef Vermicelli (page 146), but you can also use it simply, on eggs or in dips for fried foods. Store it in the refrigerator for up to three months after opening.

Kim Tu Thap Saigon Pancake Flour Mix

This mix is the base ingredient of the batter to make

Vietnamese sizzling pancakes, or Bánh Xèo (page 77). You'll just need to add coconut milk, spices, seafood, and vegetables to the mix, as instructed in the recipe.

Kim Tu Thap Tempura Batter Mix

We use a mix to make tempura batter for deep-fried dishes like Salt and Pepper Calamari, or Mực Rang Muối (page 91), as well as for the lobster in our Lobster Special (page 186). There's no need to make your own, as this version, readily available online and reliable, will meet all your needs. When frying with this batter, don't worry about a bit of clumping as it will help you achieve the desired fluff and crisp around your seafood. Wrap in plastic wrap or place in an airtight zip-top bag and store in a cool, dry place such as a pantry for up to two weeks after opening.

Lee Kum Kee Oyster Sauce

A thick, rich, and salty paste made with oyster extracts, oyster sauce is a slightly sweet and umami-rich seasoning often used for stir-fried dishes. The OG oyster sauce maker, Lee Kum Kee is said to have accidentally invented the condiment in 1888. In Vietnamese cuisine, it's often used to balance lemongrass-heavy dishes. We use it in our Lemongrass Beef Vermicelli (page 146), our Lemongrass Chicken (page 172), and our Beef in Betel Leaf (page 95). Store in the refrigerator for up to a year after opening.

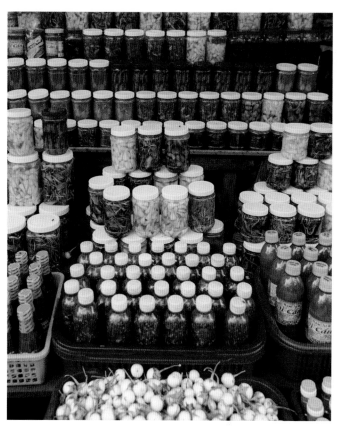

Markets in Saigon boast a range of fresh, pickled, and dried goods that serve as building blocks to Vietnamese cuisine.

Maggi Seasoning Sauce

Though it was invented in Switzerland in the nineteenth century, Maggi Seasoning Sauce has fascinatingly become popular across numerous cuisines, including Vietnamese. Often compared to soy sauce for its color and taste, it's actually a vegetable protein concentrate that offers a punchier vegetable taste, described as a mix of celery, parsley, and fennel. It's a great flavor enhancer on plain rice, baguettes, eggs, and of course proteins, like our Shaking Beef, or Bò Lúc Lắc (page 169). The umami kick of the sauce also makes it great for splashing into soups, sauces, and curries. Maggi is often sold in a glass bottle, with a red and yellow label. Store in a cool, dry place such as a pantry for up to two years after opening.

Monosodium Glutamate (MSG)

We use MSG in dozens of dishes in this cookbook, and we're not shy about it! A compound officially named monosodium glutamate, MSG is a staple across Asian cuisines, used to give any dish a big kick of umami. MSG is produced by the fermentation of starch, sugar beets, sugarcane, or molasses. Our preferred brand is Ajinomoto, which offers a high-quality MSG and cute bottles as well. Store in a cool, dry place such as a pantry for up to one year after opening. Note: In the past, MSG was commonly misunderstood as unhealthy due to its presence in processed foods. Because of this, MSG and by extension mom-and-pop Asian restaurants that used it were often viewed as low quality. However, today, MSG is generally recognized as an important ingredient (and is deemed by the FDA as safe for consumption). And no Vietnamese kitchen is complete without it.

Pearl River Bridge Mushroom-Flavored Superior Dark Soy Sauce

While fish sauce is more quintessentially Vietnamese, soy sauce makes its way into Vietnamese cooking, thanks to a strong historic Chinese influence. Our preferred brand is Pearl River Bridge's superior dark soy sauce, which is the most flavorful variety. It's a great all-purpose soy sauce with a rich profile and earthy mushroom flavor. Store in a cool, dry place such as a pantry for up to one year after opening.

Shrimp Paste

Made by grinding fermented ground shrimp (like those shown below), shrimp paste is often referred to as the stinkier cousin of fish sauce, in that both are made from fermented seafood and offer a hit of umami to Vietnamese dishes. It's also, admittedly, one of the ingredients that non-Vietnamese diners sometimes find overpowering. In this cookbook, we only use it for our central Vietnamese noodle soup, Bún Bò Huế (page 135), for which it is an essential ingredient. We use Lee Kum Kee's finely ground shrimp paste, but you can use what is readily available to you (it typically comes in a small plastic container or glass jar and can be ordered online). Store in the refrigerator for up to three months after opening. Because of its strong aroma, be sure to seal it tightly before storing.

Sriracha

Sriracha is an iconic hot sauce typically made with a combination of chile peppers, vinegar, garlic, and sugar. Though it has roots in Thailand, it is most associated in America with the brand Huy Fong. It's typically used as a condiment for phở (pages 123, 129, and 132) and other soups, though it can also be used as a dip for any fried food as well. At Madame Vo, we make our own, but we also stand by the tried-and-true Huy Fong version, which can easily be identified by its rooster logo, bright red-orange hue, and green squirt top. If you can't find it, try the Kikkoman or Tabasco versions. Store in the refrigerator for up to a year after opening.

LEFT: dried shrimp RIGHT: shrimp paste

NOODLES: Noodles are one of the fundamental building blocks of Vietnamese cuisine, and we employ many varieties. Here are the noodle types you'll encounter in this cookbook. As a general note: for rice noodles, we typically use the fresh variety in soup-based dishes, and use the dry variety for stir-frying, as fresh noodles tend to clump together when fried. However, dry noodles are totally usable for any of our recipes. For all noodles, make sure to refer to the package instructions for guidance on cooking them to perfection.

Bean Thread Noodles / Miến

Also sometimes referred to as cellophane noodles or glass noodles due to their transparent appearance, bean thread noodles are thin, long noodles made from mung beans. They are used in our Egg Rolls, or Chả Giò (page 79).

Egg Noodles / Mì

Made from wheat flour and eggs, mì, or egg noodles, are typically used in Chinese-influenced dishes. There are different levels of thickness that distinguish types of egg noodles. For our Mì Xào Giòn Hải Sản (page 144), we use the thinner chow mein noodles since they're fried to a crisp. Meanwhile, for our Lobster Special (page 186), we use the thicker, heavier lo mein noodles that are comparable to an Italian bucatini pasta.

Rice Stick Noodles / Bánh Phở

Bánh phở is a flat rice noodle made simply from rice flour and water. Though sizes vary a bit, they are similar to the broad rice noodles used in pad Thai. As the name implies, they are used in the various styles of phở noodle soup dishes, including our Beef Phở (page 129) and Chicken Phở (page 132).

Rice Paper / Bánh Tráng

Though not technically a "noodle," rice paper is also made from rice, is often served alongside grilled meats (page 94), and is used to make various rolls such as Gỏi Cuốn (page 84). A thin, translucent wrapper, it comes dried in a package and is rehydrated within seconds. It is typically circular in shape and functions as a tortilla or wrap does in other cuisines.

Rice Vermicelli Noodles / Bún

Another type of rice noodle, bún refers to vermicelli, which are usually rounder and thinner than bánh phở noodles. Bún is often used in cold noodle salads, like Bún Thịt Nướng (page 165) as well as in hot noodle soups, like Bún Bò Huế (page 135).

Tapioca-Rice Noodles / Hủ Tiếu

Hủ tiếu is a Chinese-influenced noodle type made with cassava or yuca flour for a texture that's bouncier than rice noodles. In terms of thickness, it falls between bánh phở and bún. The most common Vietnamese dish made with this noodle is Hủ Tiếu Nam Vang, a Chinese Cambodian–inspired noodle soup, as well as its similar counterpart from the Mekong Delta region of Vietnam, Hủ Tiếu Mỹ Tho (page 137), which is featured in our book.

Rice noodles, egg noodles, and rice paper at a market in Ho Chi Minh City's Chinatown neighborhood in District 5, taken in March 2024

HERBS & OTHER FRESH INGREDIENTS:

Herbs are prized in Vietnamese cuisine, elevating nearly all dishes with complexity, fragrance, and balance. Some, like lemongrass, are used as ingredients for soups and stir-fries, while others like cilantro, mint, Thai basil, and Vietnamese coriander are often served fresh in plentiful quantities as garnishes for noodle dishes and fried foods. The great variety of herbs is a result of Vietnam's diverse climates, from tropical in the south to temperate in the north and central regions. The use of herbs, along with dipping sauces, is a hallmark of Vietnamese food.

When served as garnishes, herbs are meant to be used interactively and according to personal preference. You may choose to use a leaf of lettuce and some leaves of fresh mint to wrap around a fried egg roll. Or you can tear leaves off a sprig of basil and put them directly into your bowl of noodles. The point is that everyone has their favorite herbs, and everyone eats them differently and in varying quantities.

We recognize that a few of these herbs might not be sold at your local American supermarket, but if you have an Asian supermarket, they definitely will be. When unable to acquire a tough-to-find herb, like, say, Vietnamese coriander, you can substitute the more common ones like cilantro, mint, and basil. Or consider purchasing dried varieties, which are readily available online and must simply be rehydrated.

There may be some additional herbs needed for specific recipes in this book, but the following are the most important ones to know.

Chives / Hẹ
Chinese chives, also known as garlic chives, are tubular green leaves used as both a vegetable and an herb in Vietnamese cooking. Unlike European chives, which have a more onion-forward profile, they have a stronger note of garlic, hence the name.

Cilantro / Rau Ngò
This pungent and citrusy herb is used in soups, salads, and condiments. Integral to many of Vietnam's most beloved dishes, cilantro leaves are added by the handful to phở and bún chả. Cilantro pairs well with ingredients like fish sauce, garlic, and chiles.

Garlic / Tỏi
This pungent and aromatic bulb is used in marinades, stir-fries, and soups. A staple ingredient in Vietnamese cooking, garlic is featured in dishes such as cơm tấm, a grilled pork dish that is typically served with broken rice and a side of garlic-infused fish sauce, and chả giò, or Egg Rolls (page 79), filled with ground pork, vegetables, and spices. We also use Crispy Fried Garlic (page 63) as a key garnish for rice and noodle dishes.

Ginger / Gừng
This warm, slightly spicy root is valued for its bold flavor and medicinal properties. Some popular Vietnamese dishes that feature ginger include Bún Bò Huế (page 135), a spicy beef noodle soup that is flavored with a blend of lemongrass, chiles, and ginger, and Chicken Salad (page 102). Ginger is also

Ginger, shallots, and other aromatics on display at a street market in Ho Chi Minh City, also called Saigon

used to add a subtle kick to Vietnamese stir-fries.

Green Onions / Hành Lá
Also called scallions, green onions are central to Vietnamese food, where they are often used as a refreshing, aromatic garnish. Green onions are found at all supermarkets, sold in bunches. We'll use chopped raw green onions throughout the book, and they also appear in the recipe for a rich condiment, Green Onion Oil (page 55).

Lemongrass / Sả
A widely used ingredient in Vietnamese cuisine that is valued for its refreshing, lemony flavor and fragrance, lemongrass is usually finely chopped or pounded into a paste to be used in soups, dipping sauces, curries, stir-fries, and marinades. Popular dishes that use it include grilled chicken (page 172) and beef (page 146) and phở (pages 129 and 132), where it complements fish sauce, garlic, star anise, ginger, and other savory, aromatic ingredients. Lemongrass can be stored in the refrigerator wrapped in damp paper towels for up to two weeks.

Mint / Húng Lủi
This vibrant, refreshing herb is valued for its cooling properties in salads, soups, and meat dishes. Some popular Vietnamese foods that feature mint include Gỏi Cuốn (page 84), a type of fresh spring roll that is filled with shrimp, pork, rice vermicelli, cilantro, and mint, and Bún Thịt Nướng (page 165), a grilled pork and noodle dish that is served with a side of mint, Thai basil, and cilantro. In Vietnamese salads, mint is combined with other fresh vegetables such as cucumber, carrot, and lettuce. You may tear off the leaves and discard the stem, or serve the mint on the stem.

Pandan / Lá Dứa
This verdant leaf is often referred to as the "vanilla of Southeast Asia," as it is used in Thai and Vietnamese desserts and drinks to impart a subtle

sweet flavor, as well as an eye-catching green color. If you have the leaves, it's very easy to make pandan extract from scratch, as we do in our recipe for Pandan Sticky Rice (page 218). However, for some recipes, like our Honeycomb Cake (page 214), we call for store-bought pandan extract as it works better with the texture. If you can't find the leaves, you can use the store-bought version wherever it is called for.

Shallots / Hành Tím

This sweet, mild onion is frequently used in Vietnamese stir-fries, soups, stews, sauces, and marinades. Dishes that include shallots range from our Vietnamese Savory Turmeric Pancake (page 77), a crispy pancake that is filled with shrimp, pork, and bean sprouts, to Canh Chua Tôm (page 107), a tangy sour soup with shrimp, pineapple, and tamarind. Shallots pair particularly well with Vietnamese ingredients like fish sauce, lime juice, and chiles.

Thai Basil / Húng Quế Thái

A sweet and slightly spicy herb with hints of anise and mint, it adds an element of freshness as a garnish or flavoring agent in stir-fries and noodle dishes, such as phở or bún chả. Thai basil is typically added simply as a garnish toward the end of the cooking process due to its delicate flavor that can easily be overwhelmed by other ingredients. You may tear off the leaves and discard the stem, or serve the basil on the stem.

Vietnamese Coriander / Rau Răm

Referred to as Vietnamese coriander (but also sometimes Vietnamese mint), rau răm is a spicy, musky, and citrusy herb that adds depth of aroma and flavor to many dishes, like our Grilled Razor Clams (page 181) and Chicken Salad (page 102). Vietnamese coriander is available in most Asian supermarkets and is worth seeking out for its distinctive taste. If you can't find it, mint or Thai basil can work in a pinch.

A typical selection of herbs, vegetables, and fruit at a market in Saigon

The most traditional pickled condiment in Vietnamese cuisine is the combination of carrot and daikon radish, which are thinly sliced and soaked in vinegar and sugar. The pickles are then tucked into Vietnamese sandwiches (pages 124 and 127) and used to top rice noodle bowls, like our Grilled Pork Vermicelli (page 165). In fact, đồ chua is so iconic we knew it had to be the first recipe in this book. Traditionally, both the carrot and daikon radish are thinly sliced, but we prefer to cube the radish as shown for a contrast of textures.

.PICKLES.

Pickled Vegetables
Đồ Chua

Makes 1 quart (960 ml)

Method

Use a mandoline to julienne the carrots nice and thin, or for more crunch you can cut the carrots into thicker matchsticks, as shown here, using a knife. Cut the daikon into dice-size pieces.

In a medium saucepan over medium heat, heat the vinegar, mirin, and sugar, stirring until the sugar has dissolved. Remove from heat and transfer to a large bowl to let cool to room temperature (about 30 minutes).

Add ¼ cup (60 ml) water. Mix in the fennel seeds. Add the carrots and daikon and mix to combine.

Immediately transfer the mixture to a sealed jar or airtight container and refrigerate for at least 1 day and up to 1 month. The longer you keep it, the more concentrated the flavor becomes.

Ingredients

½ pound (225 g) carrots, peeled

4 ounces (115 g) daikon radish, peeled

½ cup (120 ml) white vinegar

¼ cup (60 ml) mirin

¼ cup (50 g) sugar

½ tablespoon fennel seeds

THE ICONIC COMBO: PICKLED CARROTS AND DAIKON RADISH

Pickled vegetables, or đồ chua (which literally translates to "sour stuff"), are essential to a Vietnamese kitchen. Typically used as garnish, they add a sweet and sour crunch to a wide range of dishes—and can also be snacked on alone. Growing up, my parents always had jars of pungent, pickled stuff around, and my friends were known to ask, "What is that smell?" It was a funny, only-in-an-Asian-household moment.

SAUCES

Vietnamese Dipping Sauce
Nước Mắm Chấm

Makes 1 quart (960 ml)

Fish sauce, made from fermenting anchovies, is considered the mother condiment of Vietnamese cuisine, and is the source of umami for many of our dishes. The simplest way to use it is in nước chấm (which literally means "dipping sauce"). The combination of fish sauce with lime juice, garlic, and chile is known for its perfectly balanced mix of sweet, sour, salty, spicy, and savory flavors. This beloved concoction can be found on every table in Vietnam—and is used as an all-purpose accompaniment to hundreds of dishes. And even though it's called a dipping sauce, don't let that name hold you back. Nước chấm also can be poured directly over savory foods like grilled meats, or used as a very pungent salad dressing. We even eat it just with rice and a fried egg. We keep a gallon-size jug in our refrigerator at all times, and if you try this dipping sauce, you might start doing the same.

Ingredients

8 to 10 red Thai chiles (based on spice preference), chopped

1¼ cups (250 g) sugar

¾ cup (180 ml) fish sauce, such as Three Crabs

¼ cup (60 ml) distilled white vinegar

1 cup (255 g) minced garlic (approximately 48 cloves, which you can mince in a mini food processor)

½ teaspoon monosodium glutamate (MSG)

Juice of 1 lime

Method

Using a mortar and pestle, crush the Thai chiles and set aside. (If you do not have a mortar and pestle, smash the chiles with the flat side of your knife.)

In a small pot over medium heat, add ½ cup (120 ml) water and the sugar and stir. Once the sugar has dissolved, immediately transfer to a medium mixing bowl and add the crushed Thai chiles, fish sauce, vinegar, garlic, MSG, and lime juice. Whisk to combine with chopsticks and adjust as needed to achieve your preferred balance of sweet and spicy. Store for up to 2 weeks in an airtight container in the refrigerator; the flavor concentrates pleasantly the longer you let the sauce sit.

Tamarind Sauce
Nước Chấm Me

Makes about 1½ cups (355 ml)

Tamarind is an underrated ingredient in Western cuisine that plays a big role in Vietnamese cooking. It offers a sour, fruity taste to balance this sweet sauce that's particularly delicious in combination with grilled meats and vegetables. In Vietnam, the pulp of the tamarind is dissolved in water, but we use a tamarind concentrate here. We use this as a dip for our Beef in Betel Leaf (page 95), or when making rice paper rolls with Grilled Meats (page 94). Or, even if you're having a non-Vietnamese barbecue at home, this sauce can add a kick to your meats.

Ingredients

¾ cup (150 g) sugar

3 tablespoons honey

¼ cup (60 ml) tamarind concentrate, such as Cock Brand Concentrate Cooking Tamarind

3 tablespoons chili sauce, such as Huy Fong Chili Garlic Sauce

6 to 8 red Thai chiles, diced

½ cup (120 g) minced garlic

10 tablespoons (150 ml) fish sauce, such as Three Crabs

Method

Add 1 cup (240 ml) water to a 2- to 3-quart (2- to 3-L) saucepan and bring to a boil. Stir in the sugar and honey.

Once the sugar and honey have dissolved, take the pan off the heat, pour the mixture into a medium mixing bowl, and add the tamarind concentrate, chili sauce, and Thai chiles. Stir for 3 minutes. Add the garlic and fish sauce and stir with chopsticks for 2 minutes. Let sit for at least 15 minutes to allow the flavors to meld.

Use immediately or refrigerate in an airtight container for up to 2 weeks.

Tamarind Sauce (left) and Chili Sate Sauce (right)

Not to be confused with the peanut-based Indonesian sate sauce, Vietnamese sate sauce (shown opposite) is a secret weapon in our kitchen. A type of Vietnamese chili oil, this condiment packs just the right amount of heat while adding lots of bold umami flavor from its use of garlic, chile peppers, and a hint of fragrant lemongrass. Its wide use in Vietnamese cuisine is visible in the bright red hue it adds to dishes like soups and skewers. Use it anywhere you would use a hot sauce: we like it on our Mama Ly's and Papa Ly's Fried Rice (pages 148 and 149), but you can also use it on fried eggs, steaks, and soups.

Chili Sate Sauce
Ớt Sa Tế

Makes 1¼ cups (285 ml)

Method

Preheat a 2- to 3-quart (2- to 3-L) saucepan over medium heat, then add the oil and garlic. Stir for 2 to 3 minutes, until the garlic is golden brown, then immediately add the lemongrass. Stir constantly for 2 to 3 minutes, until the lemongrass is golden.

When the lemongrass becomes fragrant, turn off the heat. Add the shallots, Thai chiles, Korean pepper flakes, turmeric, MSG, sugar, and salt. Stir everything together and then simmer the mixture over low heat for 2 to 3 minutes.

Let cool to room temperature and serve, or store in an airtight container for up to 2 weeks (there is no need to refrigerate it).

Ingredients

6 tablespoons (90 ml) vegetable oil

1 tablespoon minced garlic

½ cup (55 g) minced lemongrass (about 1½ stalks)

3 tablespoons sliced shallots

1 tablespoon chopped red Thai chiles

3 tablespoons coarse Korean red pepper flakes, such as Chaeun

1½ teaspoons turmeric powder

1 tablespoon monosodium glutamate (MSG)

2 tablespoons plus 1½ teaspoons sugar

1 tablespoon kosher salt

COUNTERCLOCKWISE FROM TOP: Vietnamese-Cajun Orange Butter (page 52), Madame Vo Green Seafood Sauce for Seafood, Mama Ly's Seafood Sauce (page 53).

Almost every Vietnamese family has at least one sauce recipe that isn't entirely traditional, an original creation that becomes a household staple. For us, this was a sweet and creamy but also fresh cilantro-based sauce that my mom loved at an event and immediately tried to re-create at home. According to her, it's a French-influenced dipping sauce that's ideal for seafood, like our Salt and Pepper Calamari (page 91), or vegetables like fried taro, or even just French fries. The mayonnaise adds richness, while the cilantro and vinegar cut through fried flavors well. Many of our customers have asked us for this recipe—and now you have it.

Madame Vo Green Sauce for Seafood

Makes 3 cups (750 ml)

Method

Add ½ cup (120 ml) water to a 2- to 3-quart (2- to 3-L) saucepan and bring to a boil. Add the sugar and stir to dissolve. Remove from the heat and let cool.

In a food processor, combine the celery, jalapeño, cilantro, avocado, mayonnaise, salt, MSG, and vinegar, followed by the cooled sugar water. Puree for 3 to 4 minutes on high to a silky-smooth consistency.

Use immediately or store in an airtight container in the refrigerator for up to 1 week.

Ingredients

½ cup (100 g) sugar

3 stalks celery, chopped

1 jalapeño chile, sliced

½ bunch cilantro, chopped with stems

½ ripe medium avocado, halved, pitted, and peeled

½ cup (120 ml) mayonnaise, such as Hellman's

1½ teaspoons kosher salt

½ teaspoon monosodium glutamate (MSG)

¼ cup (60 ml) distilled white vinegar

Vietnamese-Cajun Orange Butter

Makes about 1 quart (960 ml)

Our orange butter pays homage to Vietnamese-Cajun food. From Houston to New Orleans, the Gulf Coast area has a huge Vietnamese population. Vietnamese-Cajun crawfish, which has become hugely popular over the last decade, is different from the classic Cajun version in that the crawfish is tossed in seasoning after it's boiled, which coats the shell and adds tons of flavor. It's also served with a dipping sauce that typically includes butter and often citrus wedges like lemon and orange. I tried this for the first time in Houston and knew I wanted to make a version that I could use at home in New York, where crawfish aren't so easy to find, for dipping any seafood like lobster, crab, and shrimp.

Ingredients

Vegetable oil

½ cup (120 g) minced garlic

1 pound (455 g) unsalted butter

7 tablespoons (90 g) sugar

2½ teaspoons ground black pepper

2 teaspoons monosodium glutamate (MSG)

2 tablespoons salt

1 large orange, ½ zested, juice squeezed and reserved

Up to 1 tablespoon hot sauce, such as Tabasco (optional)

Method

Preheat a 2- to 3-quart (2- to 3-L) saucepan to medium heat and add 2 tablespoons oil. Once the oil has heated, add the garlic and cook for 2 to 3 minutes, until fragrant and golden. Reduce the heat to medium low, then add the butter and gently stir until melted. Add the sugar, pepper, MSG, and salt and stir for 2 to 3 minutes. Finally, add the orange juice and stir until evenly combined.

Turn up the heat to high for about 1 minute, until the mixture starts bubbling. Then, immediately turn off the heat and gently stir to combine. Add the orange zest and up to 1 tablespoon hot sauce, if you prefer some spice.

Serve the sauce immediately or store in an airtight container in the refrigerator for up to 1 week and warm before serving.

This seafood-friendly dipping sauce is my mom's signature creation, making use of key Vietnamese ingredients like kumquats, sweetened condensed milk, and fish sauce. Kumquats are often used in seafood dishes because they help bring out the flavor of grilled fish, prawns, and lobster. The sweetness of the condensed milk helps balance out the tart citrus. You can use this as an all-purpose seafood dipping sauce, whether you're making a recipe from this book or enjoying another dish like your favorite fried seafood or seafood boil.

Mama Ly's Seafood Sauce

Makes ½ pint (240 ml)

Method

Cut the kumquats into quarters and remove the seeds.

In a food processor fitted with a blade attachment, add the kumquats, ¼ cup (60 ml) water, lime juice and leaves, garlic, condensed milk, fish sauce, Thai and jalapeño chiles, and sugar.

Puree on high speed for 3 minutes, or until a silky-smooth consistency is achieved.

Serve immediately or store in an airtight container in the refrigerator for up to 2 weeks.

Ingredients

3 kumquats

Juice of 1 lime

10 lime leaves

4½ tablespoons (70 g) minced garlic

6 tablespoons (90 ml) sweetened condensed milk, such as Longevity

6 tablespoons (90 ml) fish sauce, such as Three Crabs

4 red Thai chiles

3 to 4 jalapeño chiles

5 tablespoons (65 g) sugar

Vietnamese Peanut Sauce
Tương Chấm

Makes about 1 cup (240 ml)

This peanut dipping sauce is the designated accompaniment to fresh Spring Rolls, or Gỏi Cuốn (page 84). The combination of hoisin, peanut butter, and chili sauce adds an instant hit of nuttiness, sweetness, and spice to the freshness of the roll. The fact that gỏi cuốn is one of the most popular appetizers found on Vietnamese restaurant menus in America indicates that this sauce is widely beloved by association.

Ingredients

2 tablespoons vegetable oil

3 cloves garlic, minced

½ cup (120 ml) hoisin sauce, such as Lee Kum Kee or Koon Chun

1 tablespoon chili sauce, such as Huy Fong Chili Garlic Sauce

1 tablespoon peanut butter

2 tablespoons crushed roasted peanuts

4 red Thai chiles, sliced (optional)

Method

Heat a medium saucepan over medium heat. Add the oil. After 30 seconds, add the garlic and stir to keep it from burning. After another 30 seconds, add the hoisin sauce, chili sauce, and peanut butter.

Immediately add 1¼ cups (300 ml) water and let the mixture simmer until it thickens, about 2 minutes.

Pour the sauce into a bowl. Let it cool and then top with the roasted peanuts and Thai chile slices, if using. It can be stored in a small airtight container in the refrigerator for up to 1 week.

Green onion (or scallion) oil is a staple of Asian cuisine that is a snap to make. It is a welcome addition to pretty much any rice or noodle dish, but especially to those that feature a grilled meat, such as our Grilled Pork Vermicelli (page 165) and Grilled Pork Chop Over Rice (page 167). Because Vietnamese food rarely uses butter, scallion oil is a way of adding richness along with an herbal and fragrant element that is in line with the Vietnamese culinary ethos.

Green Onion Oil
Mỡ Hành

Makes ¾ cup (180 ml)

Method

Preheat the vegetable oil in a medium saucepan over high heat.

Once the oil is hot, add the green onions, lower the heat to medium, and stir for 1 minute. Add the sugar, MSG, and salt and mix to combine; immediately turn off the heat to avoid burning the green onions, which should remain soft and green in color. Use while hot or cool to room temperature.

We recommend making this fresh every time you want to serve it, but you can store it in an airtight container in the refrigerator for a maximum of 2 days. Bring to room temperature before serving.

Ingredients

½ cup (120 ml) vegetable oil

1 bunch green onions, cut into rounds

1 teaspoon sugar

½ teaspoon monosodium glutamate (MSG)

1 teaspoon kosher salt

Vietnamese Pâté (page 59),
Vietnamese Mayo (page 58) with a
bánh mì and its other key ingredients,
like Pickled Vegetables (page 45),
Vietnamese ham, chiles, and herbs

Vietnamese Mayo

Makes 16 ounces (480 ml)

Vietnamese mayo is the most crucial ingredient in bánh mì sandwiches (pages 122, 124, and 127), tying the flavors of the pickled vegetables, fresh herbs, and proteins together. There is no bánh mì without Vietnamese mayo. Growing up, we ate these sandwiches once a week, and making the accompanying mayonnaise is still one of my mom's biggest joys. It's her recipe that we used at our family restaurant, Paris Sandwich—and still use today. This mayo is special because of the large number of egg yolks, which make it slightly yellow in color and extra rich. Besides Vietnamese sandwiches, you can use it anywhere you would use regular mayonnaise: It's as beautiful on a bagel as it is on a baguette.

Ingredients

5 large egg yolks

2 cups (480 ml) vegetable oil

5 tablespoons (80 g) minced garlic

1½ teaspoons kosher salt

1 tablespoon sugar

1 tablespoon ground black pepper

Method

Set up a stand mixer with a whisk attachment. Whisk 2 of the egg yolks on the highest setting, and then slowly pour in 1⅔ cups (400 ml) of the oil while continuing to whisk. This process should take around 2 minutes. Don't pour the oil too fast: The goal is for the ingredients to gradually bind together and thicken.

Lower the mixer setting to medium and add the garlic, salt, sugar, and pepper. Continue to mix for 3 to 4 minutes, allowing the ingredients to bind and the color to become light yellow.

Increase the mixer setting to high and add the remaining 3 egg yolks and ⅓ cup (80 ml) oil. Mix for 3 to 4 minutes, until a thick and buttery consistency is achieved, with a more golden-yellow color.

Store the mayonnaise in an airtight container (you can use a 16-ounce/480-ml deli container) in the refrigerator for up to 2 weeks.

This is a pork and chicken liver pâté that is typically made for Vietnamese sandwiches, or bánh mì (pages 122, 124, and 127), where it pairs beautifully with Vietnamese Mayo (opposite), savory meats, fresh herbs, and pickled veggies. However, in my family, we keep pâté in our refrigerator at all times for a quick breakfast or a late-night snack with bread or crackers.

It was really tough getting this recipe out of my mom because it's her pride and joy. It's the version we used at our family restaurant, Paris Sandwich, and she spent years perfecting it. We still use this pâté today as part of the Vietnamese charcuterie board at Monsieur Vo (you're welcome to use it in your charcuterie boards too!).

For the pork liver in this recipe, check out your local Asian super-market or you can special order it from a good butcher.

Vietnamese Pâté

Makes 18 ounces (510 g)

Ingredients

8 ounces (225 g) pork liver, cut into 1-inch (2.5-cm) pieces

8 ounces (225 g) chicken liver, cut into 1-inch (2.5-cm) pieces

2 cups (480 ml) milk

3 shallots, minced

12 cloves garlic (about 1 medium head), minced

2 tablespoons kosher salt

8 ounces (225 g) pork fat (lard), cut into 1-inch (2.5-cm) pieces

¼ cup (60 ml) vegetable oil

½ teaspoon five-spice powder

1 tablespoon freshly ground black pepper

3 tablespoons sugar

1 large egg

1 tablespoon monosodium glutamate (MSG)

recipe continued

Method

Rinse the pork and chicken liver, pat the pieces dry with a paper towel, and place them in a medium bowl. Add the milk and let the liver soak. After 30 minutes, pour out the milk, discard it, and rinse the liver thoroughly again. The milk gives the pâté a creamy texture.

In another medium bowl, use a wooden spoon to mix the shallots, garlic, salt, and pork fat.

Heat a 12-inch (30-cm) frying pan over medium-high heat and add the oil. Add the liver, seasoned pork-fat mixture, five-spice powder, pepper, and sugar and sauté for 3 to 4 minutes, until golden brown. Set aside to cool for 10 minutes.

Place the liver mixture in a blender and add the egg and MSG. Mix on the puree setting until a smooth consistency with no large chunks is achieved. This will take 4 to 5 minutes, depending on the power of your blender.

Line an 8 by 4-inch (20 by 10–cm) loaf pan with parchment paper. Pour the blended pâté mixture into the loaf pan and cover it with foil.

Fill a 12-inch (30-cm) steamer basket with water and heat over high heat. When the water begins to release steam, place the loaf pan into the steamer and cover. Steam on high heat for 1½ hours, or until the pâté mixture begins to solidify.

Remove the pâté from the steamer and let cool for 2 to 3 hours to harden further. Refrigerate the pâté in the loaf pan for an additional 2 hours before using. Once hardened, use a flat wooden scraper spoon or spatula to scoop it out.

The pâté can be stored in an airtight container (we recommend dividing it between two 8-ounce [240-ml] deli containers to avoid overpacking it) in the freezer for a month, or in the refrigerator for 1 to 2 weeks.

Fried shallots are used as a garnish for dozens of Vietnamese dishes, from salads to rice dishes, soups, and more. We'll call for them often in the recipes in this book, including the Chicken Salad (page 102), Grilled Pork Vermicelli (page 165), and My Tho Noodle Soup (page 137). I sometimes even add them to my sandwiches. While you can buy them (Wangderm makes good ones), they are better homemade. It's great to always have some on hand, like all Vietnamese families do, because they add great flavor and texture to every dish.

Crispy Fried Shallots
Hành Phi

Makes 1 cup (55 g)

Method

Cut the shallots crosswise into even rings using a mandoline or a sharp knife.

In a medium saucepan, heat the oil to medium heat or around 300°F (150°C) when measured with an instant-read thermometer. Place the sliced shallots in the hot oil and stir continually with large cooking chopsticks to separate the shallot rings and help cook them evenly on all sides. Fry for 5 minutes, or until golden brown.

Once the shallots turn golden, remove them from the oil immediately using a slotted spoon and place them on a paper towel to absorb excess oil.

Serve immediately or store the shallots in an airtight jar or container for up to 2 weeks (they can be left out at room temperature; no need to refrigerate).

Ingredients

4 shallots, peeled, ends trimmed

¾ cup (180 ml) vegetable oil

Bà Hoa Market in Bình Tân District, Saigon

Like our Crispy Fried Shallots (page 61), fried garlic is a topping to sprinkle generously on a variety of Vietnamese dishes, like Rice Cakes Pan-Fried in Egg (page 85), Chicken Salad (page 102), and Tết Noodles (page 140). For this recipe, and really all of our recipes, it's very important to use fresh cloves of garlic rather than anything pre-minced, as the preservatives in pre-minced garlic alter the flavor.

Crispy Fried Garlic
Tỏi Phi

Makes ⅓ cup (35 g)

Method

In a medium saucepan, heat the oil to medium heat, about 3 minutes. Add the garlic and fry for 3 to 4 minutes, or until light golden, stirring periodically with large cooking chopsticks.

Use a fine-mesh strainer to separate the garlic from the oil. Spread out the garlic on a paper towel for at least 5 minutes to soak up excess oil.

Once cool, the oil in the pan can be reserved in an airtight container for future cooking, as it is infused with the flavor of garlic.

Store the crispy garlic in an airtight jar or container for up to 1 month (it can be left out at room temperature; no need to refrigerate).

Ingredients

½ cup (120 ml) vegetable oil

20 cloves garlic (about 1½ medium heads), peeled, smashed, and minced

Salt, Pepper, and Lime Dip
Muối Tiêu Chanh

Makes a generous ¼ cup (70 g)

This is the simplest condiment on the Vietnamese table: an equal parts combination of salt and pepper, plus a sprinkle of MSG and the juice of a lime (or some calamansi, if you have access to this tiny lime). It can be used as a dip for a variety of proteins ranging from beef, like our Shaking Beef (page 169), and seafood, like our Grilled Razor Clams (page 181).

Ingredients

2 tablespoons kosher salt

2 tablespoons ground black pepper

½ teaspoon monosodium glutamate (MSG)

1 lime

Method

Put the salt, pepper, and MSG in a large ramekin, then squeeze in the juice of the lime. Use a small spoon to stir until all the ingredients are mixed. Do not store this; make it fresh every time.

Chile Salt for Fruit
Muối Ớt Chấm Trái Cây

Makes a generous ¼ cup (80 g)

This simple, three-ingredient blend makes a world of difference for fruit, especially the juicy tropical fruits found in Vietnam. The spice works to bring out the sweetness of mango, pineapple, guava, and citrus, such as pomelo. This tastes particularly delicious when the fruit is not so sweet yet, and is still somewhat ripe, crunchy, and sour.

Ingredients

3 red Thai chiles, roughly chopped

¼ cup (60 g) kosher salt

½ teaspoon sugar

Method

Use a mortar and pestle to pound the Thai chiles until flat. Add the salt and sugar, then continue pounding for 2 minutes, or until the mixture is a brown-orange color.

Serve immediately in a ramekin alongside a plate of your favorite fruit.

Chile Salt for Fruit

Chapter II
Starters • Salads • Soups
(Plus Stews and Curry)

A VIETNAMESE KID FROM QUEENS

Why I Rep NYC All Day

Family outing where we toured Ellis Island and the Statue of Liberty and took in views of the Twin Towers, 1994

I was born in 1985 at St. Vincent's Hospital in the West Village, and I was raised in Jackson Heights, Queens, which is notable for being the most ethnically diverse urban area in the world. They call it "the world's borough." And true enough, growing up, my friends came from all over the world; they were Asian, Latino, Black, white. And yes, the food in my neighborhood was just amazing. Though our restaurant is in the heart of Manhattan, I will forever represent Queens, which is where my family and I still live today.

My earliest memories as a kid revolve around my parents working themselves to the bone to get our family on our feet. We had rented a two-bedroom apartment in Jackson Heights, and I remember seeing dad when he'd come home late from work. Since the early eighties, he'd worked his way up from being a dishwasher to being a chef at Chinese restaurants all over New York, from Queens to the Upper East Side. He continued this for a decade, before finally quitting to help my mom, who was growing her nail business.

When I was born, my mom worked in New Jersey, where she was learning to do nails. Throughout my early years, she stayed there during the week, and I only saw her on the weekends. It was just me and my dad at home. Later, she opened her first salon in Astoria on Thirtieth Avenue, close to Steinway Street, a famous eating destination lined with global restaurants. By the time I was in college, her one shop had become six.

One of my mom's loyal customers, Carmen, became my godmother. Carmen was originally from Madrid, Spain. She introduced me to foods like beans, fried pork chops, and empanadas. She also taught me what it meant to be American. Since my family didn't celebrate Western holidays like Easter and Thanksgiving, it was Carmen who taught me how to commemorate these days and understand what made them special. I wanted to tell this story because I'll never forget that.

Since my parents worked long hours, I didn't see as much of them as I would have liked, if I'm being totally honest. But around the time I turned ten, my parents decided to make Sundays our family day and market day. So as a kid, I cherished the time I got to spend with them going to the seafood market, the meat market, and the Asian supermarket. This is where my dad taught me to choose a ripe watermelon by knocking on it and listening for a hollow sound. Then there was grapefruit—I learned to feel the weight of the citrus in my hand to assess its meatiness. With durian, I'd check the rivets and lumps. I learned so many techniques I still use today.

In the kitchen, I'd help my parents prepping for events and parties. At times, I hated the never-ending bustle. Every weekend, there would be another party. And for me, it was always "pluck these string beans" or "wash these dishes." Cooking for our guests was my mom's thing—her pride and joy—and being the only child, I wanted to impress my parents. On regular weeknights, cleaning the rice and cooking it was my job. My mom would call me on her way home from work to prep meat. At the beginning, I fucked up a lot: The meat wasn't properly thawed; the rice was too wet. And I would get my ass handed to me.

I won't say it was glamorous, but I think these experiences—and getting yelled at constantly—helped me thrive in a real-world restaurant setting. By the time I was eight, I was experimenting on my own, starting, of course, with things like instant noodles. Two of my cousins who were close to my age lived down the street. When we'd get out of school, our parents would still be working. So we'd go to my home and I'd whip up some weird creation for us—playing around with spices and MSG. I had no idea what I was doing: Once, I burned an egg because I didn't know you needed to put oil on the pan first. We had no internet, no instruction. Trial by error was a great teacher.

With their hard work, sweat, and tears, my parents gave me all the tools I needed to one day open Madame Vo. In addition to a love for food, they also gave me my business acumen: At a young age, I was running the cash register at my mom's nail salon, learning how to interact with customers and how to execute a basic transaction. Running a business is in my blood.

Culturally speaking, my mom and dad were pretty typical Asian immigrant parents. They wanted me to understand the value of hard work, but never wanted me to have to do the same kind of manual labor they did. In traditional Vietnamese culture, education is the highest virtue. So even though we were a Buddhist family, my parents enrolled me at the local private Catholic school. Though my mom knew very little about the American education system, she'd asked all her well-manicured clients where they sent their kids. That's where she decided to send her son.

I know that I'm blessed to have grown up in New York City. My only experiences with racism were the soft kind of mockery that adolescent boys inflict on one another. Admittedly, the other kids used to call me "pork fried rice," but I never felt the same kind of outsider status that so many others knew.

On the other hand, Yen grew up in Long Beach, Mississippi—as deep South as it gets. Though there were refugee enclaves elsewhere in Mississippi, such as Biloxi, Yen tells me she and her family were some of the only Vietnamese immigrants in her immediate area, and that she always felt the need to speak English and bring American food to school. After all, at this time, down in Texas, Vietnamese fishermen were still being attacked openly by the KKK.

If there was one thing that I missed growing up in New York City, it was a strong connection to Vietnamese culture and community. Although New York City has a fantastic, widespread Chinese community, I only knew of a few small Vietnamese neighborhoods in the Bronx and Brooklyn. And while it's true that I identify as both Chinese, from my dad's side (see page 73), and Vietnamese, and speak both languages, I've always felt a deeper longing for a connection to my Vietnamese identity.

After all, Vietnamese is the language both my mom and dad share, and at home, we typically ate more Vietnamese food than any other kind. In Jackson Heights, I made friends from China, Thailand, and all over Asia—but I was often the lone Vietnamese kid. I would always ask myself, "Am I Vietnamese? Am I Chinese? Or am I just American?" And it's perhaps because of this that I became especially proud to be Vietnamese. I've always had a strong passion for the culture, and deep respect for what we have been through as a community.

On Regionality in Vietnamese Cooking

From the country's northern region, which emphasizes savory and clean flavors, to the southern region, which prefers sweet and strong seasonings, it's hard to overstate how diverse Vietnamese palates and ingredients can be. In addition to food, accents vary across different Vietnamese regions.

Even with an iconic national dish like phở, there are differences between the northern and southern styles. For example, northern phở, or phở bac, is typically clear and minimally seasoned and garnished, resembling a consommé that is light but soul-warming as a breakfast. Meanwhile, southern phở is known for its rich broth

Bún bò Huế is the signature lemongrass-flavored Central Vietnamese noodle soup dish of Huế.

and generous accoutrements like Vietnamese coriander, cilantro, and sliced chiles. It's a hearty meal.

At Madame Vo, because both of our families are from Saigon, we identify most closely with southern Vietnamese cooking, which usually makes use of big and bold flavors. The Vietnamese term we like to use is "đậm đà," which literally translates to "rich" or "warm." Our phở (pages 129 and 132) represents this flavor profile.

While our focus is on the south, you'll find dishes from each of the three main regions of Vietnam in this book:

Northern Vietnam
In northern Vietnam, and especially in the capital, Hanoi, food is prepared with an emphasis on the harmony of salty, sweet, and sour. Iconic dishes of the north include chả cá (fish cakes with dill) and bún chả, a noodle dish with grilled pork patties—popularized worldwide when the late Anthony Bourdain and President Obama shared a meal together in Hanoi.

Central Vietnam
Central Vietnam, characterized by its highland terrain as well as being the seat of the former imperial court in the city of Huế, differs most from both the lowland regions of northern and southern Vietnam—both in terms of linguistics and cuisine. Speakers of the various Central Vietnamese accent groups are notoriously tricky

to understand for north and south Vietnamese people, and the food is likewise distinct in its use of fermented fish sauce, shrimp paste, and a wide variety of chile peppers. Our book includes a recipe for Huế's signature soup, a lemongrass beef vermicelli noodle soup (page 135).

Southern Vietnam
Southern Vietnam, which includes Saigon, is defined by its tropical climate and proximity to the Mekong Delta region, which offers a bounty of rice, fruits, fresh herbs, coconuts, and sugar. Dishes unique to the south include hủ tiếu (see page 137), a Chinese and Cambodian–influenced noodle dish, and the original Vietnamese bánh mì sandwich (see pages 122, 124, and 127).

On Being Chinese-Vietnamese

LEFT: My dad, chairman of the New York Chao Chiu Association
RIGHT: My mom with my dad's dad, who passed his Teochew heritage to me

Beyond the diversity in culture and cuisines attributed to geography, Vietnam is an ethnically diverse country too. While the Kinh people make up more than 85 percent of the population, there are fifty-four recognized ethnicities in Vietnam. The ethnic Chinese, who are called Hoa people in Vietnamese, make up 1 percent. Many of the Chinese in Vietnam are specifically Teochew (in Vietnamese: Triều Châu), which refers to a distinct people and language who come from the Chaoshan region of eastern Guangdong province. I grew up speaking many dialects and languages, but primarily Teochew and Vietnamese.

My dad was very proud to be Triều Châu, and he instilled this in me. I remember when we would go visit his family in Australia, he would remind me to only speak Triều Châu to my grandparents. I never forgot the importance of passing along language as part of our culture—today, my and Yen's kids can also speak Triều Châu, in addition to Vietnamese.

Understandably, there's always been some tension between the two sides of my culture: As it turns out, my father's family wasn't initially onboard with my dad marrying a Vietnamese girl. Today, they've come around, loving and accepting my mother as part of the family, but I was always fascinated with how this cultural identity influenced older generations.

The legacy of our mixed heritage has also impacted my cooking because, as a chef, my dad would often make Chinese food—he always missed the food from his region growing up. And even when we made Vietnamese food at home, my mom would tend to find a compromise on the flavors, allowing both cultures to come together on the plate.

From Madame Vo's menu, the Bánh Bột Chiên (page 85), or crispy rice cakes fried in egg, is one prime example of a Chinese-influenced Vietnamese dish because the rice cakes are very Chinese and the dish is topped with Chinese sausage. But with the introduction of egg and the fish sauce used for dipping, it becomes distinctly Vietnamese.

And our Garlic Noodles (page 143) also come from my dad. These showcase both Chinese and Cambodian influences, since my father is Chinese but grew up in Cambodia. The noodles are inspired by hủ tiếu noodles, which are called kuyteav in the Cambodian language, Khmer; however, for our version, we use rice noodles because we prefer the texture.

Funny story: When Yen met me, she discovered that she is also part Triều Châu, through her grandfather. She didn't know this but, one time, when I heard her speaking to her aunts, I realized she was using a Chinese word for "auntie." The whole time, she thought she was just speaking Vietnamese!

Madame Wings
Cánh Gà Chiên Nước Mắm

Serves 4 to 6

This best-seller at Madame Vo comes from Papa Vo's side of the family. Yen's father would make these marinated and double-fried wings every year for Super Bowl parties. We love sports, and so we take our game-day food seriously. Seasoned with fish sauce and chili garlic sauce, they're a dependable crowd-pleaser. While this dish is very easy to make, it's packed with flavor and embodies our cooking in its purest form with the holy trinity of Vietnamese ingredients: fish sauce, garlic, and sugar.

Ingredients

Vegetable oil, for frying

12 chicken wings, medium to large drumettes or flats (flats are crispier; about 18 ounces / 510 g)

6 cloves garlic, minced

1 tablespoon fish sauce, such as Three Crabs

1 tablespoon chili sauce, such as Huy Fong Chili Garlic Sauce

¼ cup (50 g) sugar

Pinch ground black pepper

1 tablespoon sliced green onion, cut on a bias

Method

Fill a medium saucepan halfway with oil and bring to high heat. When the oil starts to gently bubble, reduce to medium heat, 375°F (190°C) when measured with an instant-read thermometer.

Pat the chicken wings dry with a paper towel and then, without coating or dredging the wings, deep-fry them until crisp, about 15 minutes. Remove using tongs or large chopsticks and set aside.

Reheat the oil until it reaches 450°F (230°C). Fry the wings again for 3 to 4 minutes (for double the crispiness).

Heat a large nonstick frying pan or wok over high heat and add 2 tablespoons oil. When the oil starts to spread evenly across the bottom of the pan, add the garlic and the fried wings and toss until the garlic is light brown and fragrant. Lower the heat to medium low.

Add the fish sauce, chili sauce, sugar, and black pepper. Continue tossing the wings until the sauce caramelizes, 2 to 3 minutes.

Serve the wings immediately topped with the green onion.

Bánh xèo is a Vietnamese savory turmeric pancake that is filled with pork and shrimp, then folded in half. Once when my parents were preparing for a party, I completely burned a bánh xèo. I got chewed out so badly, I've never forgotten it. As I got better at cooking, this dish represented a challenge that I overcame. Today, I take pride in the traditional version we serve at Madame Vo, which is a customer favorite. Despite this commonly used name, don't expect the texture of a regular pancake here: These are crispy and fried.

Since you'll only be able to fit one pancake per pan, there is not an easy way to cook these pancakes in large quantities. At home, we typically make them all quickly, one after another, and eat them right away. So be sure to prep all your accompanying herbs and sauces ahead of time, so you can just fry and enjoy the bánh xèo immediately. To keep the pancakes warm as you're making more, you can make a few and stack them on top of one another.

Vietnamese Savory Turmeric Pancake
Bánh Xèo

Makes 4 large pancakes (serves 8 to 10)

Ingredients

FOR THE PANCAKE BATTER:

1 (12-ounce/340-g) bag Kim Tu Thap Saigon Pancake Flour Mix

1 (14-ounce/400-ml) can coconut milk, such as Aroy-D

1 teaspoon kosher salt

2 teaspoons turmeric powder

2 green onions, thinly sliced

1 (12-ounce/360-ml) can club soda

FOR THE FILLING:

Vegetable oil, for frying

1 pound (455 g) pork belly, thinly sliced into ¼-inch (6 mm) strips

1 pound (455 g) colossal prawns (about 13 to 15), peeled and chopped

¼ cup (60 g) minced garlic

2 tablespoons fish sauce, such as Three Crabs

1 tablespoon sugar

¼ teaspoon ground black pepper

1 teaspoon monosodium glutamate (MSG)

8 ounces (225 g) jumbo lump crabmeat

8 ounces (225 g) mung bean sprouts

1 red onion, thinly sliced

FOR THE GARNISH:

1 head leaf lettuce

1 bunch mint

1 bunch basil

Pickled Vegetables (page 45), as garnish

Vietnamese Dipping Sauce (page 46)

recipe continued

Method

Make the pancake batter: In a large mixing bowl, combine the pancake flour mix, coconut milk, salt, turmeric powder, green onions, and club soda. Whisk to evenly combine and achieve a silky texture; set aside.

Make the filling: In a frying pan, bring 3 tablespoons of oil to high heat. Sear the pork belly until it starts to crisp, about 5 minutes, before removing it to a plate. Then sear the shrimp. Once the first side is browned, flip them over and brown the second side; this should take 2 to 3 minutes total. Add the garlic, fish sauce, sugar, black pepper, and MSG. Stir to combine, then add the pork and crab and stir again to combine. After cooking for about 5 minutes, remove the filling from the heat to a bowl and set aside.

1.

2.

3.

Fry a pancake: Evenly coat a medium nonstick frying pan with a thin layer of oil and bring it to high heat. Using a 3-inch (7.5-cm) ladle or a liquid measuring cup, scoop up ½ cup (120 ml) of the batter {1} and pour it onto the pan while rotating it {2}, so the batter evenly coats the pan, forming a pancake about 12 inches (30 cm) in diameter. Lower the heat to medium low and leave for 10 minutes, or until the pancake batter ingredients start to bind. Add 3 tablespoons of the filling to cover one half of the pancake {3}. Add a handful or so of bean sprouts and onions (based on your personal preferences). Bring the pan to low temperature and fry for 5 minutes, or until the pancake starts to become crisp and golden brown. Gently fold the opposite half over the half with toppings to close the pancake up like a taco {4}.

Garnish and serve: Use a flat spatula to remove the bánh xèo and place it on a plate. Serve it immediately with lettuce, mint, basil, and pickled veggies. Invite everyone to use the lettuce to wrap up pieces of the pancake along with herbs and pickles, and then dip their wrap into the nước chấm sauce.

Repeat or store: Fry and serve additional pancakes one by one, until you have used up the remaining batter. Alternatively, the batter can be stored in an airtight container in the fridge for up to up to 2 days.

4.

No Vietnamese party is complete without a tray of fresh, home-cooked fried egg rolls. If you run out, you simply haven't prepared properly. We *always* make tons of extra egg rolls to keep frozen for emergencies. One key difference between the Vietnamese and Chinese varieties is that the former typically uses vermicelli noodles and wood ear mushrooms as filling, and you'll mostly find cabbage in the latter. Take note: You will have to use your hands to make the filling–and assemble each roll individually–however, it will be well worth the effort.

Egg Rolls
Chả Giò

Makes 40 to 50 rolls

Ingredients

FOR THE FILLING:

1 ounce (28 g) shredded dried wood ear mushrooms

1 package (1.76 oz /50 g) dried bean thread vermicelli noodles, such as Pagoda Vermicelli

3 cups (330 g) peeled and shredded taro

2 cups (220 g) shredded carrots

1¼ cups (160 g) minced red onion

8 ounces (225 g) lump crabmeat

1 pound (455 g) peeled large shrimp (about 26 to 30), minced

1 pound (455 g) lean ground pork

8 ounces (225 g) ground rendered pork fat, sourced from your local butcher (optional, but it will make the rolls taste richer)

¼ cup (35 g) tapioca flour or starch

2 tablespoons kosher salt

5 tablespoons (55 g) sugar

1 tablespoon chicken bouillon, such as Totole Granulated Chicken Soup Base Mix

1½ teaspoons monosodium glutamate (MSG)

⅓ cup (75 ml) fish sauce, such as Three Crabs

3 tablespoons ground black pepper

½ cup (53 g) Crispy Fried Garlic (page 63)

FOR THE WRAPPERS:

2 (9-ounce/250-g) bags frozen wheat-based egg roll wrappers, such as Spring Home TYJ Spring Roll Pastry

2 large eggs, whisked

Vegetable oil, for frying

FOR SERVING:

Your favorite vegetables and herbs, such as lettuce, mint, and Pickled Vegetables (page 45)

Vietnamese Dipping Sauce (page 46)

recipe continued

Method

Prep the filling: In two medium mixing bowls, soak the wood ear mushrooms and vermicelli noodles separately in lukewarm water for 15 minutes until softened. Strain out all the water.

In a large mixing bowl, combine the wood ear mushrooms and vermicelli noodles with the shredded taro, carrots, red onion, crab, shrimp, pork, and pork fat (if using). Wearing gloves, evenly mix all the ingredients. Once thoroughly mixed, add the tapioca flour, salt, sugar, boullion, MSG, fish sauce, black pepper, and fried garlic. Continue to knead with your hands for 2 minutes to thoroughly combine into a homogenous mixture.

Wrap the egg rolls: Thaw the frozen wrappers, then peel them apart and stack them so you can easily pull one off at a time. Set the wrapper on your work surface so that one corner is facing you, forming a diamond shape. In that corner closest to you, add about 2 tablespoons of your filling {1}, adding a bit more or less depending on how thick you prefer the roll to be. Fold that bottom corner over the filling {2}, then fold the corner to your left inward toward the center {3}, followed by the corner to your right, to completely cover the filling {4}. Then roll up the wrapper toward the top corner to close it into a tight roll {5}. Using your fingers or a pastry brush, coat the edge of the wrapper in whisked egg and press down firmly to seal it so the roll doesn't open during frying.

Deep-fry: To a 3-quart (3-L) saucepan, add oil to fill the pan halfway and then bring to medium heat, or around 400°F (205°C) when measured with an instant-read thermometer. When the oil starts to gently bubble, reduce the heat to medium. Place five to six rolls in the oil at a time, in order to avoid overcrowding. Fry each batch for 8 to 9 minutes, until they are floating and golden brown.

To serve: Using tongs or large cooking chopsticks, remove the fried egg rolls from the saucepan and let them drain on a paper towel. Let cool for 5 minutes before serving (I love my egg rolls piping hot, so don't wait much longer than that). To eat, you can wrap one roll in a piece of lettuce with a few leaves of mint and some pickled vegetables, then dip the whole thing in the Vietnamese dipping sauce.

To store: Wrap leftover rolls in plastic wrap, then store them in the freezer for up to 2 months. They will stick together as they freeze, but when you're ready to reheat, you can easily pull them apart and they won't break. To reheat, deep-fry them again without thawing.

1.

2.

3.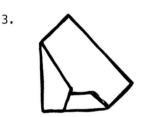

4.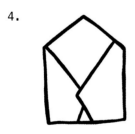

5.

Autumn Rolls
Bò Bía

Makes 14 to 16 rolls

Bò bía is a Vietnamization of the Chinese Teochew popiah rolls. But aside from the fact that both are fresh rolls filled with Chinese sausage and jicama, the rolls are pretty different. In contrast to the Teochew version, which typically uses an egg-based wrapper, this Vietnamese variety puts the egg *inside* the roll, which is wrapped with rice paper. This was a weekly dish in my household when I was growing up.

Ingredients

Vegetable oil, for frying

4 Chinese sausages (185 g), such as Kam Yen Jan Chinese-style sausage

1 pound (455 g) jicama, chopped into matchstick-size pieces

½ cup (70 g) minced garlic

½ cup (60 g) dried shrimp, such as President, roughly minced

1 tablespoon fish sauce, such as Three Crabs

2 tablespoons sugar

1 tablespoon monosodium glutamate (MSG)

¼ teaspoon ground black pepper

6 large eggs, whisked

1 (12-ounce/340-g) package dried rice paper, such as Tufoco

½ cup (70 g) crushed roasted peanuts

2 to 3 tablespoons (30 to 45 ml) Sriracha sauce, such as Huy Fong

⅓ cup (80 ml) hoisin sauce, such as Lee Kum Kee or Koon Chun

1 quart (960 ml) Vietnamese Peanut Sauce (page 54)

Method

Set a medium frying pan on high heat and add enough vegetable oil to cover the bottom of the pan (about ¼ cup / 60 ml). After the oil is hot, add the Chinese sausages and cook until they are brown and crisp, about 2 minutes. Remove the sausages but leave the oil in the pan.

In the same pan, add the jicama, garlic, dried shrimp, and fish sauce to the oil, stirring to combine, and cooking until browned, about 4 minutes. Add the sugar, MSG, and ground black pepper, periodically mixing the filling until the jicama begins to soften, about 8 minutes. Slice the cooked Chinese sausage on a diagonal and add the slices to the pan.

In a separate medium frying pan over high heat, add a little oil. When hot, add the eggs and cook, stirring occasionally, until the eggs are scrambled and look dry and well done. Set aside.

In a large bowl filled halfway with water, submerge 1 sheet of rice paper, until soft and pliable, about 2 seconds. Shake off the excess water and place the softened, wet rice paper on a plate. In the middle of the bottom third of the rice paper, add 2 heaping tablespoons of the jicama and sausage mixture, 1 tablespoon of the scrambled eggs, 1 teaspoon roasted peanuts, ½ teaspoon Sriracha, and 1 teaspoon hoisin sauce {1}. Start rolling upward from the bottom flap, making sure to keep the filling tucked in as you go {2}. Once the filling has been rolled over twice, fold the left and right sides of the rice paper in to seal the ends of the roll {3}, and then continue rolling until tight and compact {4}. The rice paper will stick to itself and naturally hold all the ingredients together. Repeat with the remaining ingredients.

Serve the rolls warm, at room temperature, or chilled, sprinkled with crushed peanuts and with peanut sauce on the side for dipping.

1.
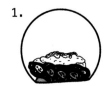

2.

3.

4.

Autumn Rolls (top left) with Spring
Rolls (see page 84 for recipe)

Spring Rolls
Gỏi Cuốn

Makes 12 to 16 rolls

The name "spring rolls" can refer to several different rolls that are either fresh or fried. At Madame Vo, however, spring rolls are fresh rolls filled with shrimp, pork belly, and vegetables wrapped in rice paper. Our Vietnamese Egg Rolls, or Chả Giò (page 79), on the other hand, are fried. Gỏi Cuốn are an excellent option when you want a fresh, crunchy, satisfying snack, no frying required. They're extremely easy to make, especially if you already have the sauces on hand. They are also fun to make with friends and family, as the rolling is interactive and not intimidating for beginners.

Ingredients

1 pound (455 g) jumbo shrimp (about 10 to 12), peeled

Kosher salt

1 pound (455 g) pork belly

4 ounces (115 g) dried rice vermicelli noodles (bún), such as Bamboo Tree

1 (12-ounce/340-g) package dried rice paper, such as Tufoco

1 head romaine lettuce, leaves separated

1 ounce (28 g) fresh Chinese chives, sliced crosswise in half

1 bunch basil

1 bunch mint

8 ounces (225 g) mung bean sprouts

Vietnamese Dipping Sauce (page 46), for serving

Vietnamese Peanut Sauce (page 54), for serving

Method

In a large pot, bring 2 cups (480 ml) water to a boil, then add the shrimp and cook until they turn pink in color, about 3 minutes. Remove the shrimp from the pot and set aside, leaving the water boiling. Once the shrimp are cooled, slice them in half lengthwise.

Rub 1 tablespoon salt on the skin of the raw pork belly. In the same pot of cooking liquid used for the shrimp, add the pork belly and cook for 30 minutes, or until tender enough to fall apart when pulled with chopsticks. Remove the pork with tongs or large cooking chopsticks but keep the water boiling. Rinse the pork under cold water to cool and pat it dry. Once the pork is cool enough to handle, thinly slice into 2-inch-long (5-cm) strips and set aside.

In the same pot (with new water), cook the rice noodles according to the package instructions. Drain, rinse with cold water, and set aside.

In a large bowl halfway filled with water, submerge 1 sheet of rice paper for about 2 seconds, until soft and pliable. Shake off the excess water and place the softened, wet rice paper on a plate. In the middle of the bottom third of the rice paper, add a palm-size clump of noodles, 2 pork belly slices, 3 shrimp halves, 1 lettuce leaf, 2 chive sprigs, 3 or 4 basil leaves, 3 or 4 mint leaves, and a handful of bean sprouts. Start rolling upward from the bottom flap, making sure to keep the filling tucked in as you go. Once the filling has been rolled twice, fold the left and right sides of the rice paper in to seal the ends of the roll, and then continue rolling until tight and compact. The rice paper will stick to itself and naturally hold all the ingredients together. (The process is the same for the Autumn Rolls. See page 82 for some step-by-step illustrations.)

Serve the rolls with the filling still warm, at room temperature, or chilled, with Vietnamese dipping sauce and peanut sauce on the side.

Bánh bột chiên is a Chinese-influenced dish made by frying rectangular chunks of rice and tapioca flour in eggs. The chewy texture of these rice and tapioca cakes makes this dish unique and hard to resist. For our version, we add coconut milk to the rice cakes for a hint of richness and buttery flavor to offset the savory Chinese sausage that tops the dish. When Yen spent her pre-NYC years in Houston, this was her go-to late-night food for after the club, served at the beloved local establishment Tan Tan.

Rice Cakes Pan-Fried in Egg
Bánh Bột Chiên

Makes 4 to 5 rice cakes
(serves 8)

Method

In a large bowl, combine the rice flour, tapioca flour, coconut milk, 3½ cups (840 ml) water, salt, and oil. Whisk until the rice cake batter is evenly combined.

Bring a nonstick 12-inch (30-cm) frying pan to medium heat. Once preheated, pour the batter into the pan **{1}** and cook for about 8 minutes, stirring constantly so the batter cooks evenly. Keep stirring until it reaches a thick Play-Doh consistency, about 2 inches (5 cm) thick. Move the batter into a 9-inch (23-cm) cake pan, lined with plastic wrap. Use your hands to pat the dough to remove any bubbles and gently smooth it to evenly cover the bottom of the pan and touch the sides. Cover the pan in plastic wrap and place it in a water-filled 12-inch (30.5-cm) steamer basket over high heat for 1 hour **{2 and 3}**. Cool the rice cake for at least 3 hours, or up to overnight, in the refrigerator. You can store the batter mixture in the cake pan in the refrigerator for up to 1 week, until you are ready to finish making the dish.

Ingredients

1 (16-ounce/455-g) bag rice flour, such as Erawan

½ (8-ounce/225-g) bag tapioca flour or starch, such as Erawan

½ (14-ounce/400-ml) can coconut milk, such as Aroy-D

1 tablespoon kosher salt

2 tablespoons vegetable oil, plus more for frying

17 ounces (480 g) Chinese sausage links (about 6), such as Kam Yen Jan, chopped

1 bunch green onions, sliced

16 large eggs, whisked

½ cup (53 g) Crispy Fried Garlic (page 63), for serving

Vietnamese Dipping Sauce (page 46), for serving

1.

2.

3.

recipe continued

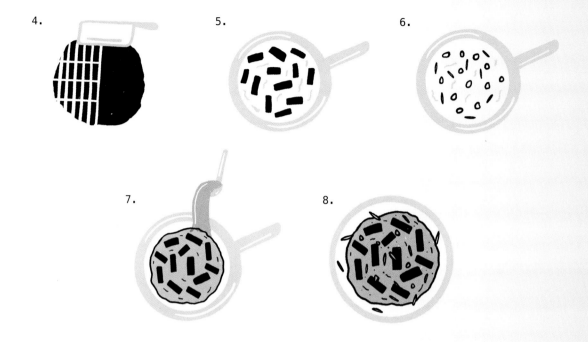

4.

5.

6.

7.

8.

Once cooled, cut the rice cake into rectangles, about 2 inches (5 cm) long and 1 inch (2.5 cm) wide **{4}**. You should have about 75 small rice cakes.

In a nonstick 12-inch (30-cm) frying pan, add enough oil to fill the pan halfway and bring the oil to medium-high heat. To avoid overcrowding, fry in batches, 12 to 18 rice cakes at a time, for 13 to 15 minutes, flipping so that all sides of the rice cakes become golden brown **{5}**. Set the fried cakes aside, on a paper towel to soak up excess oil if desired, and repeat to fry the remaining cakes.

Remove most of the oil from the pan, retaining just enough oil to coat the pan. Cook the Chinese sausage in the oil until golden brown, about 3 minutes **{6}**. Set the sausage aside on a plate.

Wipe down the pan and heat over medium heat, adding just enough oil to coat. Place 10 to 12 of the fried rice cakes in the pan, leaving about

½ inch (12 mm) between each. Pour enough of the whisked eggs over the rice cakes to just cover them (about 4 eggs / ¾ cup / 180 ml whisked eggs) **{7}**. Cook for about 1 minute. Remove the pan from the heat when the eggs have begun to set but still retain a runny texture on top. The eggs will quickly cool and congeal around the rice cakes.

Use a large spatula to carefully lift the entire egg and rice cake mixture out of the pan in one piece— it should resemble an omelet or frittata—and plate it on a large serving dish.

Use the remaining rice cakes and eggs to make additional omelets, about six to seven in all.

Top each of the omelets with the sausage and green onions, dividing the toppings evenly, and garnish with the crispy fried garlic **{8}**. Serve immediately, while piping hot, with Vietnamese dipping sauce.

FROM LEFT: Rice Cakes
Pan-Fried in Egg (page 85),
Egg Rolls (page 79), and
Papaya Salad (page 99)

Rang muối is a popular Vietnamese style of cooking seafood that translates to "salt toasted." This is our favorite way to cook squid, and it takes very little time. For our version, we use a pre-made tempura batter mix for ease, which you'll use to coat bite-size pieces of squid before deep-frying them all in hot oil. Finish by tossing them with garlic, peppers, onions, and butter for extra richness and then serve your calamari with our Madame Vo Green Sauce for Seafood (page 51) and ice-cold beer.

Salt and Pepper Calamari
Mực Rang Muối
Serves 4 to 6

Method

Butterfly the calamari by making one slice down the middle of the body and opening the tube so the inside of the body is facing up. Using the tip of a sharp knife, make diagonal parallel cuts halfway through the calamari, ⅛ to ¼ inch (3 to 6 mm) apart, taking care not to cut all the way through. Score another set of parallel lines across the first set at the opposite angle, creating a crisscross pattern. Then, using the crisscross pattern as a guide, cut the calamari into small (3-inch/8-cm) squares.

In a large mixing bowl, coat the calamari evenly with the tempura flour.

In a medium saucepan, add enough oil to fill the pan halfway and bring to high heat. When the oil starts to gently bubble and reaches 350°F (175°C) when measured with an instant-read thermometer, add the battered squares of calamari and fry for 4 to 5 minutes, until golden brown and curled. Remove the fried calamari and place on a paper towel to drain the excess oil.

Heat a large nonstick frying pan over high heat and add 2 tablespoons oil. When the oil is hot, add the garlic and fry it until golden brown, stirring frequently so the garlic does not burn. Add the red and green bell peppers, white onion, and green onions and toss for 2 minutes.

Add the fried calamari and butter to the pan, coating the calamari with the butter as it melts. After another minute, add the salt, black pepper, MSG, and sugar. Toss evenly for 2 minutes and serve immediately.

Ingredients

1 pound (455 g) whole calamari

½ cup (50 g) tempura flour, such as Kim Tu Thap Tempura Batter Mix

Vegetable oil, for frying

6 cloves garlic, minced

½ red bell pepper, with seeds and ribs removed, chopped into strips

½ green bell pepper, with seeds and ribs removed, chopped into strips

½ white onion, chopped

4 green onions, cut crosswise into quarters

3 tablespoons unsalted butter

1 tablespoon kosher salt

2 teaspoons ground black pepper

1 teaspoon monosodium glutamate (MSG)

1 teaspoon sugar

Shrimp Skewers
Chạo Tôm

Makes 10 skewers

Shrimp cakes are served in coastal areas throughout Asia. In central and southern Vietnam, a popular variation combines fresh-caught shrimp with pork paste–which comes frozen in Asian supermarkets–skewered on sticks of lemongrass (or sugarcane), then deep-fried for a deliciously sweet and savory bite. To create a full meal or fun snack platter, we serve these Shrimp Skewers and our Beef in Betel Leaves (page 95) with a platter of herbs, lettuce, fresh and pickled vegetables, plain rice vermicelli noodles, and also bánh hỏi noodles–also known as "rice vermicelli sheets." These noodles come in woven matted sheets, which allows them to be wrapped flat around meat, inside of lettuce and other herbs for additional texture.

Ingredients

1 pound (455 g) jumbo shrimp (about 11 to 15), peeled

3 ounces (85 g) frozen pork paste, such as Que Huong Nem Nuong

1 tablespoon fish sauce, such as Three Crabs

2 green onions, minced

1 tablespoon sugar

½ teaspoon ground black pepper

2 teaspoons pork stock powder, such as Knorr Pork Bouillon Mix

Vegetable oil, for frying

8 (4- to 5-inch / 10- to 13-cm) pieces fresh lemongrass or sugarcane

Vietnamese Dipping Sauce (page 46), for serving

Your favorite vegetables and herbs, such as lettuce, mint, and cucumbers (as pictured), and Pickled Vegetables (page 45), for serving

Method

Grind the shrimp in a food processor, starting on the low setting and gradually transitioning to high speed for 2 minutes until completely puréed. In a medium bowl, combine the ground shrimp, pork paste, fish sauce, green onions, sugar, ground black pepper, and pork stock powder. Let the combination marinate for 15 to 20 minutes.

Coat your hands with vegetable oil to prevent sticking and wrap about 2 tablespoons of the shrimp mixture around the top half of each stalk of lemongrass or sugarcane.

In a 3-quart (3-L) saucepan, add enough vegetable oil to fill the pan halfway and bring to medium heat, so that the oil reaches 325°F (165°C) when measured with an instant-read thermometer. Place 3 to 4 skewers into the saucepan at a time, in order to avoid overcrowding, and cook for 2 to 3 minutes. The skewers will float to the top when done. Using a spider or large cooking chopsticks, remove the skewers and set on paper towels for 2 minutes to drain off excess oil.

Serve them while hot with Vietnamese dipping sauce and the vegetables and herbs.

Rice Paper Wraps

We like to wrap grilled meats and fried foods, including many of the starters in this section like the Beef in Betel Leaf (opposite), in rice paper, as shown below. To make a wrap, submerge 1 sheet of rice paper in a large bowl halfway filled with water, for about 2 seconds, until soft and pliable. Shake off the excess water and place the softened, wet rice paper on a plate. In the middle of the bottom third of the rice paper, add some fresh herbs, pickled vegetables, and one or two of the Beef in Betel Leaf rolls (or other filling). Start rolling upward from the bottom, making sure to keep the filling tucked in as you go. Once the filling has been rolled over twice, fold in the left and right sides of the rice paper to seal the ends of the roll, and then continue rolling until tight and compact—the rice paper will stick to itself and naturally hold all the ingredients together. The roll can then be dipped in your favorite sauce. This rolling technique is also relevant to making the Spring Rolls (page 84) and Autumn Rolls (page 82) and serving any of the meats made with our Grilled Meats Marinade (page 162).

Vietnamese grilled beef wrapped in betel leaves are little rolls of smoky, savory goodness. These heart-shaped tropical leaves, also known by the name *Piper sarmentosum*, are native to Southeast Asia; they offer a distinctive peppery note and spicy aroma. On a trip to Saigon, I loved this street food, and then I played around with the recipe at home to re-create the flavors from memory–and this is the result. If you can't find betel leaves at your local Asian market, try grape leaves instead, which are tangier but not quite as fragrant, and are often found in both Middle Eastern and Asian grocers.

Beef in Betel Leaf
Bò Lá Lốt
Serves 6 to 8

Method

Make the beef: In a large bowl, add the fish sauce, garlic, lemongrass, sesame oil, oyster sauce, white pepper, star anise, chopped shallots, vegetable oil, and sugar. Mix until the sugar dissolves, then let the marinade settle for 1 minute. Add the ground beef to the bowl. Using your hands, knead the beef to incorporate the marinade. Cover with plastic wrap and let marinate in the refrigerator for 3 hours.

Make the betel leaf wraps: Rinse the betel leaves under cool water and gently pat them dry with a paper towel. Pluck all the leaves from their stalks and stack them like paper sheets on top of one another.

Place a leaf with the top side facing down on a flat work surface. Use a tablespoon to add a little of the marinated beef mixture to the bottom half of the back of the leaf. (Leaves may vary in size, so the amount of beef can vary as well.) Roll the leaf around the beef starting from the bottom. If the leaf doesn't want to fold up once you've wrapped it, use a small piece of ground beef to bind the edge of the leaf to itself. Repeat with the remaining leaves and beef filling. This will yield about 30 to 35 rolls, depending on how big they are. If you prefer to freeze some to be cooked later, freeze them in an airtight container for up to 1 month. To cook the frozen rolls, thaw them completely and then grill them.

Heat a gas grill on high for 4 minutes, then lower the heat to medium. Grill the rolls for 8 minutes until the beef is cooked, rotating periodically.

Assemble and serve: Serve the rolls while hot, topped with crushed peanuts and alongside rice paper, lettuce leaves, mint, and pickled vegetables to make wraps and tamarind sauce for dipping.

Ingredients

FOR THE BEEF:
⅓ cup (80 ml) fish sauce, such as Three Crabs

½ cup (120 g) minced garlic

5 tablespoons chopped lemongrass

⅓ cup (80 ml) sesame oil

½ cup (120 ml) oyster sauce, such as Lee Kum Kee

2 teaspoons ground white pepper

4 whole star anise, toasted

½ cup (70 g) chopped shallots (about 3 ounces)

½ cup plus 3 tablespoons (135 ml) vegetable oil

⅔ cup (135 g) sugar

2 pounds (910 g) ground beef (70% lean, 30% fat)

FOR THE BETEL LEAF ASSEMBLY:
3 pounds (1.5 kg) betel leaves

½ cup (70 g) crushed peanuts

1 head leaf lettuce

1 bunch fresh mint, stems removed

½ cup (60 to 80 g) Pickled Vegetables (page 45)

Tamarind Sauce (page 48)

Fried Shrimp Fritters
Bánh Tôm

Makes 26 to 30 fritters
(serves 8)

A popular street food in the capital city, Hanoi, these fritters combine shrimp with taro and red yams–starchy root vegetables that can easily be found at international or Asian markets. Enjoy these hearty appetizers wrapped in fresh vegetables and herbs. Yen's mom always brought these to church on Sundays, since they travel well and are easy to eat while standing.

Method

In a large bowl, add the flour, cornstarch, salt, MSG, ground black pepper, green onions, and 1¼ cups (300 ml) water. Whisk the batter together until it thickens and the ingredients are fully incorporated, then add 1 teaspoon vegetable oil and whisk again.

In a 3-quart (3-L) saucepan, add enough vegetable oil to fill the pan halfway and bring to high heat, 350°F (175°C), when measured with an instant-read thermometer.

On a flat side of a metal spatula, add about a tablespoon each of taro and yam matchsticks {1}. Dip the spatula into the oil for 1 second to fry the root vegetables, then lift the spatula out and add about a 3-inch (7.5-cm) diameter clump of batter on top of the taro and yam {2}. Use the spatula to submerge the taro, yam, and batter mixture in the oil to bind them together. Use chopsticks to slide the fritter off the spatula into the oil and continue to fry until the taro, yam, and batter are fried solidly together, about 1 minute. Remove the fritter from the oil.

Add 1 teaspoon of uncooked batter on top of the fritter, then place 1 or 2 shrimp on top {3}. Using the spatula or chopsticks, carefully place the fritter back in the oil to fry until browned, about 2 to 3 minutes. At this point the shrimp will be bound to the fritter.

Use a spider or large cooking chopsticks to remove the fritter and set it on paper towels to drain excess oil. While frying, keep a close eye on the heat, doing your best to keep the oil at 350°F (175°C). Continue cooking the fritters until you've used up all the shrimp.

Serve the fritters while hot with Vietnamese dipping sauce and vegetables and herbs.

Ingredients

1 cup (125 g) all-purpose flour

¾ cup (96 g) cornstarch

2 teaspoons kosher salt

½ teaspoon monosodium glutamate (MSG)

¼ teaspoon ground black pepper

1 bunch green onions, chopped

1 teaspoon vegetable oil, plus more for frying

¾ cup (90 g) taro, peeled and grated

1 cup (125 g) red yams, peeled and cut into thin matchsticks

1 pound (455 g) head-on jumbo shrimp (26 to 30)

Vietnamese Dipping Sauce (page 46), for serving

Your favorite vegetables and herbs, such as lettuce, mint, and Pickled Vegetables (page 45), for serving

1.

2.

3.

Papaya salad is popular throughout Southeast Asia, including in Thailand, Cambodia, Vietnam, and Laos, where it is the national dish. In contrast to other papaya salads, which tend to be very spicy, Vietnamese papaya salad has lots of fresh herb flavor. Unripe green papaya, which can be found at any Asian grocery store, as well as via online retailers, is combined with mint and basil for freshness, while you can add chili sauce and a long red chile for an extra kick of spice. Golden Mountain seasoning sauce (see page 34) is another key ingredient, which adds a hint of umami.

. SALADS .

Papaya Salad
Gỏi Đu Đủ

Serves 4 to 6

Method

Make the dressing: To a small bowl, add the seasoning sauce, sugar, vinegar, garlic, lime juice, and chili sauce with ¾ cup (180 ml) water and stir to combine.

Make the salad: In a large bowl, toss the papaya with the shrimp, basil, and mint leaves. Just before you are ready to eat, pour some of the dressing over the salad until it is well coated (you will have extra). If you'd like to reserve some salad to store in the refrigerator, keep the salad mixture separate from the dressing.

To serve: Add a sprinkle of chopped peanuts, crispy fried shallots, and red chile, if using. Enjoy at room temperature or chill in the refrigerator for an hour. Serve with the extra dressing on the side.

Ingredients

FOR THE DRESSING:
½ cup (120 ml) Golden Mountain seasoning sauce

½ cup (100 g) sugar

¾ cup (180 ml) distilled white vinegar

6 cloves garlic, minced

Juice of ½ lime

½ cup (120 ml) chili sauce, such as Huy Fong Chili Garlic Sauce

FOR THE SALAD:
1 small (2 pounds / 910 g) green papaya, peeled, seeded, and cut into matchsticks

7 ounces (200 g) jumbo shrimp, peeled, deveined, and poached

½ cup (15 g) fresh Thai basil leaves

¼ cup (15 g) fresh mint leaves

FOR SERVING:
2 tablespoons finely chopped roasted peanuts

2 tablespoons Crispy Fried Shallots (page 61)

1 long red chile, finely chopped (optional)

Pomelo Salad
Gỏi Bưởi

Serves 4 to 6

Pomelo, the largest of all citruses, is native to Southeast Asia. One of our favorite salad dishes makes use of this juicy, mildly sweet-and-sour fruit by tossing slices of it in a dressing of fish sauce, lime juice, and sugar. We like to pair this refreshing dish with fried appetizers like Egg Rolls (page 79).

Ingredients

FOR THE DRESSING:

⅓ cup (75 ml) fish sauce, such as Three Crabs

3 tablespoons fresh lime juice (from about 2 limes)

3 red Thai chiles, sliced

6 tablespoons (75 g) sugar

1 teaspoon monosodium glutamate (MSG)

FOR THE SALAD:

1 large pomelo

1 pound (450 g) shredded green papaya

¾ cup (85 g) shredded carrot

1½ cups (75 g) chopped fresh mint leaves

1½ cups (80 g) chopped fresh Thai basil

FOR SERVING:

12 jumbo shrimp, peeled, deveined, and poached in salted boiling water for 2 minutes, then halved

½ cup (70 g) crushed roasted peanuts

1 cup (55 g) Crispy Fried Shallots (page 61)

Method

Make the dressing: In a small bowl, combine ⅓ cup (75 ml) water with the fish sauce, fresh lime juice, Thai chiles, sugar, and MSG. Mix until the sugar and MSG dissolve; set aside.

Make the salad: Supreme the pomelo by using a paring knife to remove the peel, pith, and membrane. Slice into 1- to 2-inch-thick (2.5- to 5-cm) triangular wedges. In a large bowl, use your hands to mix the pomelo, papaya, carrot, mint, and Thai basil until evenly combined. Due to the nature of pomelo, it will break apart into smaller pieces as shown in the photo.

Assemble and serve: Pour the dressing into a large bowl. Add the salad mixture and toss to coat. Scoop about ½ cup (40 to 45 g) of the salad mixture onto individual serving plates. Top each portion with 2 or 3 pieces of shrimp, some crushed peanuts, and crispy fried shallots. Serve at room temperature.

Chicken Salad
Gỏi Gà

Serves 6 to 8

This is a modern take on the traditional light and bright Vietnamese chicken salad, which is typically served as an appetizer with a few pieces of shredded chicken. Our version calls for a nice serving of sliced chicken thigh, so that this salad can stand in as a main course. We've found that even non-salad-lovers like this salad because the base of cabbage makes it heartier than leafy greens would. This recipe also saves you the trouble of shredding the chicken. Key herbs in this recipe include banana blossom and Vietnamese coriander, both of which you can source from an Asian supermarket. If you do not have access to these ingredients, don't worry, just leave them out; the cabbage mixed with mint, basil, and cilantro is satisfying too.

Method

Make the chicken: Pat the chicken down with a paper towel to remove excess moisture and set aside on a platter.

In a small bowl, whisk the salt, sugar, lemongrass, and butter until the seasonings are evenly incorporated, then pour the butter over the chicken and toss to coat. Cover with plastic wrap and let sit for an hour.

Bring a 10- or 12-inch (25- or 30-cm) frying pan to medium heat, add the chicken, lower the heat, cook for 7 to 8 minutes on one side, and then turn and cook for 6 to 7 minutes. Remove from the heat and set aside to cool. You don't need oil to cook the chicken, as the butter from the marinade is sufficient.

Make the dressing: Stir the minced ginger into the Vietnamese dipping sauce.

Assemble and serve: In a large bowl, combine the banana blossom, if using, cabbage, basil, mint, cilantro, Vietnamese coriander, and red onion. Use your hands to firmly massage and mix all the vegetables together, taking care to ensure even distribution of the herbs.

Slice the chicken thighs crosswise into ½-inch-wide (13-mm) strips.

For each serving, plate about ½ cup (40 to 50 g) of the salad mixture and top with about 8 strips of the chicken. Drizzle with 4 to 5 tablespoons (60 to 75 ml) of the dressing and add a sprinkle of crispy fried shallots and roasted peanuts to finish.

Ingredients

FOR THE CHICKEN:

2 pounds (910 g) boneless chicken thighs

1½ tablespoons kosher salt

2 tablespoons sugar

½ cup (50 g) chopped lemongrass

½ cup (1 stick/115 g) unsalted butter, softened at room temperature

FOR THE DRESSING:

1 tablespoon minced fresh ginger

¾ cup (180 ml) Vietnamese Dipping Sauce (page 46)

FOR THE SALAD:

1 pound (455 g) banana blossom, thinly sliced (optional)

1 pound (455 g) purple cabbage

1 bunch basil, stems removed, leaves chopped

1 bunch mint, stems removed, leaves chopped

1 bunch cilantro, stems and leaves chopped

1 bunch Vietnamese coriander, whole leaves plucked

1 red onion, thinly sliced in half-moons

FOR SERVING:

Crispy Fried Shallots (page 61)

½ cup (70 g) crushed unsalted roasted peanuts

This simple, comforting porridge is the first dish we make whenever someone in our family is sick, or when the weather starts to get chilly. Traditionally, Vietnamese chicken congee is served alongside Chicken Salad, or Gỏi Gà (page 102). I like to take a bite of the salad and then a spoon of congee, but some people scoop some salad right into their bowl and eat it along with the congee in one bite. The crunchy cabbage in the salad adds brightness and acidity to the steaming hot porridge.

·SOUPS, STEWS, CURRY·

Chicken Congee
Cháo Gà

Serves 6 to 8

Method

Make the stock and chicken: Add 12 cups (2.8 L) water to a large stockpot and bring to high heat. Add the chicken, shallots, and ginger and bring to a boil. Add the chicken bouillon, fish sauce, salt, and sugar. Reduce to medium-high heat, add the cilantro, and cook for 1 hour. Transfer the chicken from the pot into a large bowl filled with ice to cool the chicken and tighten the chicken's skin. Using a fine-mesh strainer, strain the remaining contents of the stockpot into another stockpot, and discard the solids including the cilantro, ginger, and shallots. Shred the cooled chicken and set aside.

Make the congee: If you want a more aromatic congee, toast the uncooked rice in a nonstick frying pan over high heat for 4 minutes. Add the rice to the stockpot of broth and cook on high heat for 45 minutes to 1 hour, stirring periodically so the rice does not burn. Once the rice grains begin to break down and the stock thickens, remove from the heat.

Assemble and serve: Ladle ¾ cup (180 ml) of the congee into each serving bowl and top with a handful of the shredded chicken. Garnish with green onions, cilantro, fried shallots, fried garlic, and a pinch of ground black pepper. Serve alongside the gỏi gà.

Ingredients

FOR THE STOCK AND CHICKEN:
1 (3- to 3½-pound / 1.4- to 1.6-kg) chicken

2 large shallots, cut into wedges

1 (3-inch/7.5-cm) piece fresh ginger, skin on

2 tablespoons chicken bouillon, such as Totole Granulated Chicken Soup Base Mix

3 tablespoons fish sauce, such as Three Crabs

1 tablespoon kosher salt

2 tablespoons sugar

1 bunch cilantro, roots removed, if any, leaves and stems chopped

FOR THE CONGEE:
2 cups (380 g) white jasmine rice

FOR SERVING:
1 bunch green onions, chopped

1 bunch cilantro, roots removed, if any, leaves and stems chopped

½ cup (28 g) Crispy Fried Shallots (page 61) or store-bought fried shallots, such as Wangderm

½ cup (35 g) Crispy Fried Garlic (page 63)

Ground black pepper

Chicken Salad (page 102)

Canh chua, literally "sour soup," is a tamarind-based broth dish from the Mekong Delta region that can be made with seafood, chicken, or vegetables. In contrast to the popular Thai tamarind-based soup, tom yum, the flavor profile of Vietnamese canh chua is a balance of sour and sweet as opposed to sour and spicy. The most traditional version is made with skin-on fish, but both my wife and I never liked that when we were growing up, so our moms would make this comforting dish with shrimp instead. Later, when we were first getting to know each other, we found out that we both share a nostalgic love for this soup, and we think you will love it too. The dish is topped with Thai basil as well as elephant ear, which is similar to celery but softer and more spongelike, as well as rice paddy herb, a leafy plant that offers a strong aroma of citrus. If you do not have elephant ear, you may use thinly sliced celery. And while there is no good substitute for rice paddy herb, the soup will still be tasty without it!

Sour Soup with Shrimp
Canh Chua Tôm
Serves 6

Method

Add 7 cups (2 L) water to an 8-quart (7.5-L) soup pot and bring to a boil. Add the pineapple, tomatoes, okra, tamarind soup mix, rock sugar, fish sauce, and chicken bouillon. Simmer for 15 minutes.

Add the shrimp and elephant ear. Cook until the shrimp turns pink in color, about 2 minutes.

Ladle the soup into a serving bowl and top it with the Thai basil, rice paddy herb, Thai chiles, and crispy fried garlic.

Serve with a bowl of steamed jasmine rice on the side.

Ingredients

¼ cup (55 g) 1½-inch-diced (4 cm) fresh pineapple

2 large tomatoes, quartered

10 okra, halved lengthwise

3 tablespoons tamarind soup mix, such as Knorr Tamarind

4 ounces (115 g) rock sugar

3 tablespoons fish sauce, such as Three Crabs

1 tablespoon chicken bouillon, such as Totole Granulated Chicken Soup Base Mix

10 jumbo shrimp, peeled and deveined

2 stalks elephant ear, cut 1 inch (2.5 cm) thick

1 bunch Thai basil, sliced

1 bunch rice paddy herb, chopped

3 red Thai chiles, chopped

⅓ cup (35 g) Crispy Fried Garlic (page 63)

Steamed white jasmine rice, for serving

The origins of bò kho are murky, but some believe it is Vietnam's take on French beef stew, as it resembles the classic beouf carrotes. Indeed, it was the French who introduced beef to Vietnam. And while this dish is not on our menu, it's a clear favorite in our home because of how hearty and warming it is—braised chunks of beef accented with aromatics like five-spice and brown sugar. The longer you let it simmer, the more tender the meat becomes. The stew is known for its bright red-orange color derived from ground annatto seed—available in Asian and Latin American markets—which provides both the color and a peppery flavor. It can be ladled directly onto rice noodles or served with a toasted Vietnamese baguette, as shown here. See page 109 for more on what makes these baguettes special (but if unavailable, a French baguette would be tasty too).

Beef Stew
Bò Kho

Serves 4 to 6

Ingredients

FOR THE MARINATED BEEF:
2 to 2½ pounds (910 g to 1.2 kg) boneless beef short rib, cut into 1½-inch (4-cm) chunks

2 cloves garlic, minced

3 tablespoons minced fresh ginger

5 tablespoons (75 ml) fish sauce, such as Three Crabs

2½ teaspoons five-spice powder

1 tablespoon brown sugar

1 teaspoon kosher salt

FOR THE STEW:
3 tablespoons vegetable oil

3 stalks lemongrass, tough woody part removed, 1 stalk cut crosswise into 3-inch (7.5-cm) pieces, 2 stalks minced

8 cloves garlic, minced

1 onion, quartered

¼ cup (55 g) tomato paste

5 whole star anise, toasted

2 cups (480 ml) pure coconut water or coconut juice

1 teaspoon ground black pepper

1 teaspoon chili powder

1 tablespoon paprika

2 tablespoons sugar

1 tablespoon monosodium glutamate (MSG)

1 tablespoon salt

1 teaspoon ground annatto

8 large carrots, peeled and cut crosswise on a bias into 1½-inch (4-cm) chunks

3 tablespoons chili oil, or to taste

FOR SERVING:
¼ cup (4 g) fresh cilantro leaves, coarsely chopped

½ cup (15 g) fresh Thai basil leaves

½ cup (50 g) thinly sliced onion

2 limes, cut into wedges

1 baguette, toasted

recipe continued

Method

Make the marinated meat: Toss the beef short rib with the garlic, ginger, fish sauce, five-spice blend, and brown sugar until each piece is evenly coated. Let marinate for 30 minutes.

Make the stew: In a large stockpot or Dutch oven, heat the vegetable oil over high heat. Add the lemongrass pieces and allow them to infuse in the oil for 1 minute. Add the minced lemongrass and garlic and cook for 2 minutes. Add the onion and cook until the slices become translucent, about 5 minutes. Add the marinated beef to the pot and brown it evenly on all sides. Add the tomato paste and stir until incorporated with the meat. Cook the mixture uncovered for another 5 minutes.

In a medium frying pan, toast the star anise for 1 to 2 minutes, until fragrant.

Add 6 cups (1.5 L) water, the coconut water, toasted star anise, black pepper, chili powder, paprika, sugar, MSG, salt, and annatto. Bring the mixture to a boil, reduce the heat to medium-low, and simmer, covered, for 1 hour. Add the carrots, salt, and chili oil. Simmer for another 45 minutes to 1 hour. Using a slotted spoon, remove the lemongrass stalks and whole star anise pods from the pot.

Assemble and serve: Transfer the stew to bowls and top each bowl with cilantro, Thai basil, and raw onion. Serve the stew with lime wedges and a toasted baguette.

Cà ri gà, Vietnam's most popular version of curry, stews tender chicken and potatoes in a rich and creamy coconut curry broth. A bit thinner and less spicy than Japanese or Thai curry, Vietnamese curry has a subtle, balanced sweetness and lightness. The consistency is more like a broth.

This is another staple at our home, a tradition inherited from my parents. It is great for large parties. My family loves to host, and I remember them serving this curry at just about every gathering. My dad would often want to make it the Chinese way, with duck–the method is exactly the same, so you can try it that way, if you like. Serve the stew with noodles, as shown here, or rice. Or pair it with toasted French baguettes, which are the perfect vehicle for mopping up every last drop.

Vietnamese Chicken Curry
Cà Ri Gà

Serves 4 to 6

Ingredients

1 chicken (3 to 4 pounds / 1.4 to 1.8 kg)

2 tablespoons plus 1 teaspoon kosher salt, plus more to taste

14 ounces (400 g) red curry paste, such as Aroy-D

3 tablespoons chicken bouillon

Vegetable oil, for frying

1 pound (455 g) taro, cut in 2-inch (5-cm) cubes

8 ounces (225 g) potatoes, peeled and cut in 2-inch (5-cm) cubes

1 cup (70 g) finely chopped lemongrass

20 cloves garlic, minced

4 ounces (150 g) shallots, halved then sliced lengthwise

1 teaspoon monosodium glutamate (MSG)

2 tablespoons curry powder

1 (14-ounce/400-ml) can coconut milk, such as Aroy-D

2 red onions, quartered

1 cup (240 ml) heavy cream

2 cups (400 g) sugar

Dried rice vermicelli noodles (bún), such as Bamboo Tree

1 red horn chile pepper, sliced on a bias, for garnish (optional)

1 bunch fresh cilantro, sliced

2 bunches green onions, sliced on a bias, for garnish

1 fresh red onion, sliced, for garnish (optional)

1 lime, cut into wedges, for garnish (optional)

recipe continued

Method

Rub the chicken with 2 tablespoons of the salt and let sit for 10 to 15 minutes. Pat dry with a paper towel. If the chicken still has the head and legs (as is typical at Asian supermarkets), chop off the head and legs. Then use a butcher's knife to cut the bird in half, head to tail down the middle. Then cut each half crosswise into 6 pieces, for a total of 12 pieces.

In a small bowl, stir 1 teaspoon of the salt into the curry paste.

In a large bowl, add the cut-up chicken pieces, the chicken bouillon, and 2 tablespoons of the curry paste. Mix to combine, so the curry paste and bouillon are coating the chicken evenly, cover the bowl, and allow to sit for 30 minutes to marinate.

In a 3-quart (3-L) saucepan, fill the pan with about ½ cup (120 ml) vegetable oil and bring to high heat. When the oil starts to gently bubble, deep-fry the taro and potatoes in the oil, working in batches to avoid overcrowding, until they are a nice golden brown, 6 to 8 minutes. Once done, set them aside on paper towels to soak up any excess oil.

In a large nonstick wok or Dutch oven with a lid, heat ½ cup (120 ml) oil to medium-high heat. Add the lemongrass, garlic, and shallots and sauté for 1 to 2 minutes, until fragrant. Add the marinated chicken, MSG, and curry powder, increase the heat to high, and cook for 5 minutes. Pour in 4 cups (960 ml) water. Cover the wok, reduce the heat to medium low, and simmer for 30 minutes, stirring the chicken in the liquid occasionally for even cooking. If you happened to use a larger chicken, cook for an additional 15 minutes, or until the chicken has turned white. (You can test the doneness by pulling one piece of chicken out and tearing it open, or use a meat thermometer to ensure that temperature has reached 165°F/75°C).

Add the remaining red curry paste and stir until all the chicken is colored red. Add 1 cup water and return to a boil. Add the coconut milk, reserved taro and potatoes, and onion. Adjust the lid to leave a small opening to prevent the coconut milk from boiling over, reduce the heat to medium low, and simmer for 10 minutes. The broth should be red and yellow in color and smell amazing. Finish with the heavy cream, and season to taste with salt and sugar.

Cook the noodles according to the package instructions, and serve on the side. This should take only a few minutes so the curry will stay warm.

Garnish the curry with chile pepper, cilantro, green onions, and fresh red onions and lime wedges, if you like.

The curry can be stored in an airtight container in the refrigerator for 3 to 4 days.

Brown Butter Oxtail Congee
Cháo Đuôi Bò

Serves 6 to 8

Many regions of Asia, from Korea to Japan to China, have their own take on congee, which is rice boiled in a high percentage of water until it softens to a porridge-like consistency. One of our favorite ways to serve congee appeared on the menu of our former restaurant, Madame Vo BBQ. It features boiled oxtail that melts in your mouth, along with a special brown butter fish sauce that adds some flair to what is typically a mild, everyday meal.

Method

Make the braising sauce: In a large wok or stockpot, add the vegetable oil and bring to a high heat. Add the ginger and garlic and cook for 2 to 3 minutes, until fragrant. Add the Golden Mountain seasoning sauce, dark soy sauce, five-spice powder, star anise, MSG, and 2 cups (475 ml) water and cook for an additional 2 minutes. Remove from the heat and set aside until ready to add the oxtail.

Make the oxtail: Add a big pinch of salt to a pot of water on high heat, bring to a boil, and parboil the oxtail for 15 to 20 minutes, until the meat turns slightly gray. Drain the oxtail, rinse under cold running water, and pat dry with a paper towel. Add the oxtail to the wok with the braising sauce and cook on high heat, until the sauce reaches a boil, and then reduce the heat to medium low and simmer for 2 hours, or until the meat is tender. Then, add an additional 1 cup (240 ml) water to the wok to tenderize the meat and temper the saltiness of the thickened sauce. Cook for an additional 20 minutes.

Meanwhile, make the congee: In a 6-quart (5.7-L) stockpot, bring 4 cups (960 ml) water to a boil. Add the rice and cook for 45 minutes to 1 hour over medium-high heat, stirring every 10 to 15 minutes so the rice doesn't stick to the bottom of the pot and burn. When the congee starts to bubble, reduce the heat to low, so the congee is just lightly simmering. Add the chicken bouillon and salt to the congee and simmer for an additional hour over medium heat. During this step, you can add up to 3 cups (720 ml) water to achieve the desired somewhat runny, porridge-like consistency. (Note: The congee will continue to thicken even after it is removed from the heat.)

Make the brown butter fish sauce: In a small saucepan on medium heat, cook the brown sugar, ½ cup (120 ml) water, butter, fish sauce, and pepper for 3 minutes, stirring occasionally, until thickened. Remove from the heat and set aside.

Assemble and serve: Reserve 6 to 8 tablespoons (90 to 120 ml) brown butter fish sauce, then pour the rest into the congee. Ladle ½ cup (120 ml) congee into each serving bowl and top each serving with 2 or 3 pieces of oxtail. Finish with 1 tablespoon of brown butter fish sauce per bowl and garnish with the green onions.

Ingredients

FOR THE BRAISING SAUCE:
3 tablespoons vegetable oil

¼ cup (60 g) julienned fresh ginger

6 tablespoons (96 g) minced garlic

¾ cup (180 ml) Golden Mountain seasoning sauce

¼ cup (60 ml) dark soy sauce, such as Pearl River Bridge

1 tablespoon five-spice powder

12 star anise pods, toasted

1 tablespoon monosodium glutamate (MSG)

FOR THE OXTAIL:
Kosher salt

4 pounds (1.8 kg) oxtail, sliced into 2-inch-thick (5-cm) pieces (about 16 pieces)

FOR THE CONGEE:
2 cups (380 g) white jasmine rice

2 tablespoons chicken bouillon, such as Totole Granulated Chicken Soup Base Mix

1 tablespoon kosher salt

FOR THE BROWN-BUTTER FISH SAUCE:
1½ cups (300 g) brown sugar

½ cup (1 stick/115 g) unsalted butter

1 tablespoon fish sauce, such as Three Crabs

3 tablespoons ground black pepper

FOR SERVING:
1 bunch green onions, chopped

WHEN JIMMY MET YEN

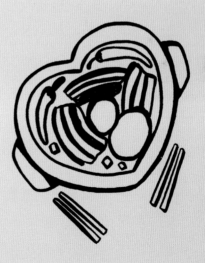

The Paris Sandwich Days

I **didn't plan on becoming a chef.** As a kid, you don't necessarily think you're going to open a restaurant one day when you grow up. So, after graduating from high school, I applied to New York University to study business. At the time, being a stockbroker or a commodities trader seemed cool to me. My parents, being frugal as they are, didn't want me to live on campus, so I commuted to school every day from Queens.

But a sinking feeling kept telling me school and a traditional office job weren't for me. Though I learned a lot in my business classes, I began to realize that I couldn't really see myself as a 9-to-5 kind of guy working behind a desk or in a cubicle. The idea of it was just demotivating, and I was progressing slowly in my studies. So, in 2004, in my sophomore year, I told my parents I'd rather go into restaurants.

Now if you know Asian parents, you know this wasn't a conversation I was eager to have. Stereotypically, our parents want us to work in traditional, prestigious jobs like "doctor" and "lawyer"—and they have no problem reminding us of the sacrifices they made to ensure that possibility. Not only that: Being a chef wasn't what it is today. You have to remember that chef culture is still very new, and back then chefs who made it to the status of "celebrity" were often white men. And my parents, who had worked their asses off doing hard labor in restaurants, couldn't imagine me doing the same.

It wasn't an easy sell. By this time, my parents were in the investment game, with dad owning real estate including a supermarket, and mom running her thriving nail businesses. Suffice to say, we were better off than we'd ever been. But they still worried that I wouldn't be able to make money or succeed. There was a lot of apprehension at first.

But as my parents have always done, they adapted. And in 2005, they began making plans to open a small Vietnamese sandwich shop called Paris Sandwich at 113 Mott Street in Manhattan's Chinatown. After helping them open it in 2006, and then operating it with them for a while, I decided to drop out of school entirely.

To get me up to speed, my parents contacted a friend in Paris who owned a bakery to ask if he would take me under his wing and teach me how to make bread. So, during the buildout of the shop, my parents sent me away to France for a couple of months to learn traditional old-world baking—with no controlled ovens and no mixers. Each morning, I'd wake up at 4 a.m. to start kneading and rolling the dough by hand, then manually proofing each batch in a cloud of steam. It was a transformative experience, and we ended up using a version of the bread I made there to create the baguettes at Paris Sandwich.

Once I returned, my mom taught me all the recipes for the fillings, and I began making all the bread. Then, we scaled it up, becoming known not just for selling delicious bánh mì sandwiches, but also supplying fresh baguettes to countless other restaurants in the city. Over time, I was tasked with managing and fulfilling all our wholesale orders. I opened and closed the restaurant daily. To be honest, I really had no life—until I met Yen.

I was introduced to Yen in August 2011 through mutual friends. Having moved to NYC from Houston, where there is a sizable Vietnamese population, I remember she was so excited just to meet another Vietnamese person. I'm pretty sure we joked about opening a Vietnamese restaurant because there were none that offered the big, bold South Vietnamese flavors we loved.

That first day we met, she asked me, "Where do you go for good Vietnamese food?" and, fatefully, I said: "My mom's house." That night, I invited her over and my mom made thịt kho trứng—a simple but iconic homestyle dish of Caramelized Pork Belly with Egg (page 175). As Yen tells it, it was love at first bite.

I continued to court Yen with food. I remember once she was craving beignets, deep-fried balls of dough topped with powdered sugar that are very typical of New Orleans and the Gulf Coast in general. So, one day when Paris Sandwich was closed at night, I invited her in and set up some aprons for a romantic baking date.

The truth is that I had never made beignets before, but I wanted to impress her, so I told her I made the best beignets. To be honest, it failed miserably: I

Our signature mural at Madame Vo, depicting a familiar face, by Michelle Matson

couldn't figure out how to make them as light and airy as they should have been. But we had a lot of fun and we still joke about it today.

For the next five years, Yen supported me every step of the way as I continued to work at Paris Sandwich. It was an incredibly difficult time.

On the business side, the Chinatown market was exceedingly competitive, with every business slashing prices in order to undercut others. And on the personal side, my parents and I began to clash over the best way to run the restaurant. My mom and dad, who came from the old-world mentality, refused to modernize and adapt. Everything had to be built, brick by brick. For example, there were

instances where I wanted to train up our staff to make some of the dishes whereas my parents felt that I should be making the dishes myself. Or, when I'd suggest adding something to the menu, they would be reluctant, since they just wanted to keep things the way they were.

There was a huge generational gap between us. And I, not wanting to let them down, abided by their desires. This led to me feeling like I couldn't become my own person and reach my full potential as a chef. Though I'm grateful that they had given me all the skills I needed to succeed, I knew that if I continued to work with them—or for them—I would not have the freedom to take advantage of this foundation.

So Yen, who had grown up more independently, and whose parents had a more relaxed approach, showed me what it meant to take control of your own life. She encouraged me to consider branching out on my own. And because she loved me for who I was, I felt supported enough to start taking this leap of faith.

We returned often to our first conversation about how there wasn't really any Vietnamese restaurant in the city that spoke to our food memories, as Vietnamese Americans who had grown up here, eating Vietnamese food at home. The vision turned into a goal we could see, and with the lease at Paris Sandwich set to end in 2016, Yen gave me some serious advice, saying I could continue to help my parents run their business on the side—but I should also set out and start something of my own.

The story of Madame Vo is, of course, a story I share with Yen. After all, she *is* Madame Vo. However, it goes deeper than that: Our major life events intertwine with important moments with the restaurant. The buildout of the restaurant took place while we were planning our wedding. Looking back, it was one of the wildest, most intense times of my life.

Our first son, Benjamin, was born in 2014. By early 2016, we felt like we had enough time to finally get around to getting married. I had been working with a realtor for months to search for a space for the restaurant. But with a wedding date confirmed, a venue in place, and caterers booked, we figured we'd put the restaurant on hold until after we paid this all off.

Life doesn't always move by your schedule. In September of that year, I found the perfect location by accident. While having lunch with a friend at Curry-Ya in the East Village, I saw that the space next door had a "For lease by owner" sign. I stood there looking at it for a good ten minutes before I called the number and asked to meet them immediately. As soon as I walked in, it felt like home. It

just felt right. That night, I stayed up all night asking myself, "Do you really want to do this?"

One day, while Yen was busy at work (she worked at an eyewear company at the time), I signed the lease. I hadn't told her I found a space and so she had never seen it. I remember calling her and her just screaming at me on the phone. Her exact words were, "Who gave you the right to sign it without me?!" Thankfully, as soon as she saw it, she was 100 percent onboard.

My parents were a little less onboard. After my fight with Yen, I then had a big fight with them. Reminding myself to trust my gut, I calmly told them I wouldn't be taking a dollar from them. At that point, I couldn't tell if they were more upset that I was striking out on my own, or that I hadn't asked them for the funds. So, we agreed to not renew the lease at Paris Sandwich. I think my parents had a really hard time seeing me grow up and not needing their help. They never trusted my vision, but this only made me even more determined to prove myself to them and their friends.

Looking back, maybe this wasn't the most financially sound plan. We had saved up for the wedding (and calculated how much we thought each of our relatives would give us for the wedding), but we were coming up short with the restaurant now included in our expenses. So, we asked everyone to put us on payment plans so we could alternate between paying off wedding bills and restaurant bills.

On October 29, 2016, Yen and I were married, and a few months later, we opened the doors to Madame Vo, on January 12, 2017.

On Bánh Mì, the Vietnamese Sandwich

In New York City, sandwiches are a big thing: from Italian subs, to chopped cheese, to lox and cream cheese on a bagel. All of these are great in their own right, but I humbly believe that Vietnamese sandwiches are unmatched when it comes to flavor and texture. There's something so comforting and satisfying about bánh mì that reminds me of home.

During my decade at Paris Sandwich, I learned how to bake bread from scratch for our bánh mì. While that's a topic for another book, what we'll teach you here is how to assemble a proper at-home bánh mì—the iconic Vietnamese sandwich created after the French introduced bread to Vietnam. The sandwich is believed to have originated with street vendors during the 1950s in Saigon, which was the capital of French Indochina at the time. (For a broader discussion of French influence on Vietnamese food, see page 24.)

The French ate baguettes as they still do today, with charcuterie-style cold cuts, cheeses, and butter. After the French left in the 1950s, Vietnamese people applied their own sensibilities, bringing in mayo and adding fresh herbs.

There are two classic styles of bánh mì (with many variations between them). The first is cold, filled with cold cuts like Vietnamese ham and head cheese. The other is hot, filled with grilled pork or chicken. Both the hot and cold versions typically accent the protein with homemade mayonnaise, fresh garnishes like cilantro and jalapeños, as well as pickled ingredients, namely daikon radish and carrot. The cold variety comes with Vietnamese Pâté (page 59), another French-influenced accoutrement that adds a ton of flavor.

The hallmark of a true Vietnamese sandwich is the bread—which is lighter and airier than the chewier French variety—as well as the use of herbs like cilantro. The thin crust allows for a big bite—with meat, herbs, and mayo—without hurting your mouth. You can find these at an Asian supermarket or Vietnamese bakery if there's one near you. And if there isn't one, you might be able to purchase a couple of loaves from a local Vietnamese restaurant that serves bánh mì. When you're unable to find a Vietnamese baguette, a French baguette works in a pinch.

Then, depending on your desired filling, head back to our recipe for Vietnamese Mayo (page 58)—or forward to our nướng recipe, a grilled meat marinade (page 162). For Vietnamese cold cuts, we also recommend buying them at your closest Asian grocer as some of the ingredients, like head cheese, may be tough to come by in mainstream supermarkets.

Or, feel free to get creative: I've stuffed an Asian baguette with our Shrimp Skewers (page 92), or fried fish and herbs and pineapple. You could also make it vegetarian with store-bought fried tofu. Yen and I love going to old Chinatown restaurants and buying just char siu pork and putting it in. And if you're really feeling like going out of the box, you can even do it with bacon, egg, and cheese. After all, bánh mì is an ever-evolving dish that has been remixed with many other cuisines—often to delicious effect.

On Phở and Other Noodle Soups

At Madame Vo, our signature dish is our namesake Madame Phở. We owe our success as a restaurant to this noodle soup, and phở is similarly essential to Vietnamese cuisine at large. For many Vietnamese people, the soup, made with rice noodles in a long-simmered stock, offers a taste of home—every family has their own recipe.

Phở, pronounced "fuh," is a rice noodle soup that features a long-simmered broth. While the protein can range from beef to chicken and vegetarian options like tofu and seitan, what makes the dish special is its use of spices like star anise, cardamom, and cinnamon to flavor the broth. The dish is typically served with the noodles, broth, and protein in the bowl with a plate of fresh herbs like Thai basil and bean sprouts alongside, which can be added to the soup based on personal preference. The typical condiments for phở include Sriracha and hoisin sauce.

The history of phở is a bit murky, but most scholars today point to early-twentieth-century northern Vietnam as the dish's birth time and place. Regardless of its precise origin, it reflects Vietnam's history, including the influence of the Chinese, who introduced noodles to Vietnam, as well as the French, who

Fresh rice noodles sold by the kilo in Saigon

popularized beef consumption. (See "On Vietnamese Culinary Philosophy and History" on page 24 for details.)

The most popular version of phở, beef phở, is often named by the specific cuts included in the broth or on the side. For example, phở tái is phở with thinly sliced eye round meat, phở bò viên is phở with beef meatballs. Ours, which might be considered a phở đặc biệt (or specialty phở, with multiple types of meat), includes eye of round, chuck short rib, beef brisket, oxtail, and rib eye steak. Looking beyond the beef versions, phở can also be made with chicken, which is called phở gà, or vegetarian, known as phở chay.

We won't sugarcoat it: Making phở from scratch is a labor of love that involves lots of prep work and multiple hours of simmering—we simmer ours for a total of 24 hours (at home, you can turn off the stove overnight for safety). We've provided our full recipe here— as we never use shortcuts with our house phở. But as fans of our most popular dish will attest, the effort is well worth it.

The good news is that you can store any extra broth—frozen for 1 month or refrigerated for 1 week—and throw it back into a pot anytime to reheat and make more phở. The fresh ingredients can be prepped ahead and kept for serving, while the noodles are best made fresh right before serving.

. BÁNH MÌ .

Grilled Pork Vietnamese Sandwich
Bánh Mì Thịt Nướng

Makes 3 sandwiches

We loved sandwiches so much that we opened up our own family sandwich shop, Paris Sandwich, in 2006. We decided to close it after a decade, but we still return to the recipes for the dishes we made there over and over again. While bánh mì can be made with cooked meat or cold cuts, this grilled pork version is my favorite and I make it at home for Yen.

Ingredients

FOR THE PORK:

1 recipe Grilled Meats Marinade (page 162)

2 pounds (910 g) pork loin, cut widthwise into 10-inch-long (25-cm) strips

2 tablespoons vegetable oil, if using a frying pan

FOR THE SANDWICH:

1 (26-inch/66-cm) baguette, toasted for 2 to 3 minutes in a hot oven

3 tablespoons Vietnamese Mayo (page 58), or more if desired

1 cucumber, cut into 4-inch-long (10-cm) spears

Pickled Vegetables (page 45)

9 sprigs fresh cilantro

3 red Thai chiles, sliced

Method

Marinate the pork: In a large bowl, combine the marinade and pork, cover in plastic wrap, and refrigerate for 2 hours or, for best flavor, overnight.

Grill the pork: Heat a gas-powered grill for 4 minutes on high. Arrange the marinated pork in a single layer on the grill, lower the heat to medium, and grill for 8 minutes on each side. Alternatively, add the vegetable oil to a 12-inch (30-cm) frying pan and bring to medium heat. Sear the meat for about 5 minutes on each side, until cooked through and golden brown.

Assemble and serve: Slice the toasted baguette crosswise into three even pieces, and then halve each piece to create the top and bottom of your sandwiches. Spread 1 tablespoon of the Vietnamese mayo on the upper half of each sandwich (but if you love mayo like Jimmy, you may want to add more, on both the top and bottom). Divide the strips of pork, cucumber spears, pickled veggies, cilantro, and Thai chiles among the sandwiches. Serve immediately.

The cold-cut version of the sandwich is the most classic type of bánh mì, typically made with Vietnamese ham (chả lụa), head cheese (giò thủ), and pork belly (giăm bông, from the French term "jambon"). We're featuring this simplified version with just the chả lụa–a ham made by steaming pork and tapioca flour seasoned with anchovy–and my mom's signature pâté, so its flavor can shine. You can find chả lụa at Asian supermarkets, typically in a roll form. It looks like a log, wrapped in a banana leaf, secured with twine. Together with the pâté, this sandwich has the perfect balance of savory flavors.

Cold-Cut Vietnamese Sandwich
Bánh Mì Kẹp Giăm Bông

Makes 3 sandwiches

Method

Slice the toasted baguette crosswise into three even pieces and then halve each piece to create the top and bottom of your sandwiches.

Spread the Vietnamese mayo on the bottom half of each sandwich and the pâté on top of the mayo.

Divide the sliced chả lụa, cucumber spears, pickled veggies, cilantro, and Thai chiles among the sandwiches. Serve immediately.

Ingredients

1 (26-inch/66-cm) French baguette, toasted for 2 to 3 minutes in a hot oven

3 tablespoons Vietnamese Mayo (page 58)

2 tablespoons Vietnamese Pâté (page 59)

4 ounces (115 g) Vietnamese ham or chả lụa, halved lengthwise, then cut into ½-inch-thick (12-mm) half-moons slices

1 medium cucumber, cut into 4-inch (10-cm) long spears

Pickled Vegetables (page 45)

9 sprigs fresh cilantro

3 red Thai chiles, sliced

The broth for our phở is based on my mom's recipe, but we also included Yen's mom's addition of a huge bone-in short rib, a twist that became somewhat of an unexpected Instagram sensation when we started posting photos of it. Because ours is a southern Vietnamese–style phở, we love exaggerating and amping up the flavors to achieve that quintessentially southern big and bold profile (for more on this, see page 72).

For example, instead of regular cane sugar, we season the broth with rock sugar, which dissolves more slowly and imparts a milder, more round sweetness. We also toast the cardinal phở spices, including star anise, cardamom, and amomi fructus (another type of cardamom, available at Asian supermarkets), then soak them in the broth for potent flavor.

In addition, we make our stock with beef bones that have been parboiled then roasted. Parboiling the bones is sufficient for a clean, pure, traditional phở. But roasting the bones creates a stock with deeper flavor.

As phở is the pride of not only our restaurant but also Vietnam as a whole, we encourage any of you reading this book to make this dish from scratch. Savoring the anticipation while preparing the ingredients and simmering the stock for hours is a labor of love and an experience that is truly Vietnamese.

NOODLES

Madame Phở
Phở Bò

Serves 8 to 12

FOR THE AROMATICS AND SPICES:
2 large white onions, halved

4 ounces (115 g) whole fresh ginger, peeled

8 shallots, peeled

8 star anise

6 whole cloves

5 cinnamon sticks

1 tablespoon coriander seeds

3 tablespoons fennel seeds

4 cardamom pods

8 whole amomi fructus (see headnote)

FOR THE BONES:
7 pounds (3.2 kg) beef bones with marrow, a mix of neck and leg bones

FOR THE BROTH:
2 pounds (910 g) oxtail, cut 1½ to 2 inches (4 to 5 cm) thick

3 pounds (1.4 kg) chuck short rib, separated into ribs

1 pound (455 g) beef brisket

Kosher salt

½ cup (120 ml) fish sauce, such as Three Crabs

3 to 4 ounces (85 to 115 g) rock sugar (depending on how sweet you like it)

FOR ASSEMBLY AND SERVING:
1 pound (455 g) rib eye steak

8 ounces (225 g) eye of round steak

2 pounds (910 g) rice stick noodles or bánh phở (these can be found dried or fresh, but we prefer a fresh variety, such as Sincere Orient Banh Phở Tuoi)

4 cups (360 g) mung bean sprouts

1 bunch cilantro, leaves and stems chopped

1 bunch Thai basil

1 bunch green onions, thinly sliced crosswise into rings

1 large red onion, thinly sliced

2 limes, cut into wedges

Hoisin sauce, such as Lee Kum Kee or Koon Chun

Sriracha sauce, such as Huy Fong

recipe continued

Method

Prepare the aromatics and spices: Char the onion, ginger, and shallots either by holding them with metal tongs over an open flame or setting them directly on an electric burner. Alternatively, you can put them on a sheet pan under a broiler. Remove after about 5 minutes, once they take on some color and char, but before they burn.

Put the charred onion, ginger, and shallots into a fine-mesh bag or wrap in some cheesecloth tied with string. (Alternatively, if you do not have either of these, just set the charred onion mixture aside, and later, when you are ready to add it to the simmering stock, carefully place on top of the phở so that you can remove the onion mixture if it begins to disintegrate into the stock.)

In a small dry pan on low heat, toast the star anise, cloves, cinnamon, coriander, fennel, cardamom, and amomi fructus for about 3 minutes, or until they begin to release their aroma (be patient and do not burn the spices).

Add the toasted spices to the bag or cheesecloth that is holding the charred onion mixture. (Or if you aren't using a bag or cheesecloth, set the toasted spices aside, and later, you can add them directly to the stock, but you will need to find and remove them before serving.)

Parboil the bones: Place the beef bones into a 10- to 12-quart (9- to 11-L) stockpot. Fill the pot with enough water to cover the bones, taking care to leave at least 4 to 5 inches (10 to 12 cm) at the top to allow room for boiling. Heat the pot on high until the water boils and let it continue to boil aggressively for 5 minutes to release impurities from the bones, then turn off the heat. Pour the contents of the pot into a colander or directly into a clean sink that is lined with a strainer to catch solids. Rinse the bones until they are clean of blood and impurities.

Roast the bones (optional): Preheat the oven to 400°F (205°C). Spread out the bones in a roasting pan or on a sheet pan with a lip to catch the fat that will be released. The marrow bones should face up so that the marrow remains intact. Roast for about 45 minutes, rotating the pan halfway through. The bones should turn golden brown. If the golden-brown color isn't achieved within this time, turn on the broiler for a few minutes to allow the bones to brown, observing carefully to make sure they don't burn. If they begin to brown too quickly, turn down the heat.

Make the stock: Put the bones into a clean stockpot. Fill the pot with water until all the ingredients are covered. Turn the heat to high but keep a close eye on the pot to prevent the water from reaching a full boil. Just before the water reaches boiling—small bubbles will begin to rise—turn the heat to the lowest setting to maintain a very low simmer for 6 to 8 hours. If you're not already using the smallest burner on your stovetop, move the pot there now to keep the heat at a minimum. You want as little movement in the water as possible. Skim the stock regularly to remove any scum and impurities that rise to the surface.

After the stock has simmered for 6 to 8 hours, use a ladle to ensure that the fat has visibly risen to the top of the broth and the collagen and marrow are no longer on the bones (the bones should be bare). Turn off the heat and allow stock to sit and cool undisturbed for 4 to 6 hours based on how much time you have, or preferably overnight. Do not cover the pot during this time.

After cooling the stock, bring it back to a boil for 1 hour, then turn off the heat. Use a spider to strain out the larger stock ingredients and discard. Strain the stock through a cheesecloth or fine-mesh strainer into a clean stockpot.

Meanwhile, preheat the oven to 375°F (190°C) and roast the oxtail on a sheet pan for about 20 minutes, until you see some browning in color and the marrow appears softer. Add the oxtail to the stockpot filled with the stock. Add the short rib and beef brisket to the stockpot raw. Bring to a boil and then turn down the heat to a low simmer. Add the charred onion, ginger, shallots, and toasted spices and simmer for 3 hours. Remove the oxtail, short rib, and brisket and set aside to cool.

Since the stock will have reduced considerably, add 2 quarts (2 L) water and season the stock with salt and fish sauce, starting in tablespoon increments and tasting as you go. The stock should end up on the saltier side, as the saltiness will balance out when served with the noodles and garnishes. Add the rock sugar, according to how sweet you like your stock. Simmer gently on low for about 10 minutes to allow the rock sugar and salt to dissolve. Leave the stock on a low simmer until ready to serve.

Assemble and serve: The rib eye and eye of round steaks should be served rare. Wrap each of these raw meats in plastic wrap and put them in the freezer for about 30 minutes, before you prepare the noodles—to let them harden a bit. This makes them easier to slice. After 30 minutes, take the meat out and slice across the grain as

thinly as possible. Refrigerate the sliced raw meat until the phở is ready to serve. Thinly slice the cooked brisket.

If using dried noodles: Use a noodle strainer basket to soak for 30 minutes in warm water or 1 hour in cold water. Add the soaked noodles to a 3-quart (3-L) pot of boiling water and cook for 15 to 20 minutes, according to package instructions. Drain the noodles and rinse under cold water; leave in the noodle strainer basket until ready to portion into bowls.

If using fresh noodles: Each bowl of noodles should be prepared individually. For each bowl, measure out 4 to 5 ounces (115 to 140 g) noodles. In a 3-quart (3-L) pot filled with about 2 quarts (2 L) boiling water, cook the noodles in batches for about 20 seconds, or until just al dente, then place them into a bowl.

Rinse the bean sprouts, cilantro, and Thai basil under cool, running water so they don't wilt immediately when added to the hot soup. Remove the eye of round and rib eye from the refrigerator. If you've made the stock ahead of time, reheat it in the stockpot. Add the meat to each serving bowl, approximately 5 slices each of eye of round and rib eye, 4 slices brisket, 2 pieces of oxtail, and 1 piece of short rib per serving.

Using a ladle, scoop about 2 cups (480 ml) stock into each bowl, being sure to submerge the noodles and meat. Top the bowl with the chopped cilantro, green onions, and red onions. On a separate plate, arrange the bean sprouts, lime wedges, and Thai basil (the basil leaves can be ripped off the stem and added directly into the broth as each person desires). Serve with hoisin sauce and Sriracha on the side, to be added based on personal preference. (Tip: Yen's favorite way to use these condiments is to squeeze both sauces into one ramekin, squeeze half a lime in, and then dip the meat into the ramekin.)

Chicken Phở
Phở Gà

Serves 6 to 8

While the traditional beef phở gets a lot of the glory, chicken phở is Vietnam's comforting and soulful version of chicken noodle soup, a favorite in many home kitchens. In my family, this dish was my mom's way of showing love. She would make chicken phở for us as a remedy for everything–from a hard day at school to a cold.

Ingredients

FOR THE STOCK AND CHICKEN:
1 (3-inch/7.5-cm) piece fresh ginger, skin-on

8 shallots (about 7 ounces / 200 g), peeled

1 chicken (2 pounds / 910 g)

1 tablespoon kosher salt, for cleaning

5 or 6 whole star anise, toasted

Large pinch coriander seeds

2 tablespoons salt

2 tablespoons chicken bouillon, such as Totole Granulated Chicken Soup Base Mix

2 tablespoons rock sugar

1 teaspoon monosodium glutamate (MSG)

2 tablespoons fish sauce, such as Three Crabs

FOR ASSEMBLY AND SERVING:
2 pounds (910 g) rice stick noodles or bánh phở (these can be found dried or fresh, but we prefer a fresh variety, such as Sincere Orient Banh Phở Tuoi)

Half a white or yellow onion, thinly sliced (about ¼ cup / 40 g)

¼ cup (10 to 15 g) sliced green onions

¼ cup (10 g) chopped fresh cilantro

¾ cup (41 g) Crispy Fried Shallots (page 61), or store-bought, such as Wangderm

6 to 8 pinches ground black pepper

2 limes, cut into wedges (optional)

8 to 10 red Thai chiles or jalapeño chiles, sliced (optional)

Method

Make the stock and the chicken: Preheat the oven to 400°F (205°C). On a baking sheet, roast the ginger and shallots for 15 minutes. When cool enough to handle, slice the ginger into quarter-size coins.

Lightly dust the chicken with 1 tablespoon of kosher salt and give it a full body scrub, then rinse it under cold running water and pat dry.

Bring a large stockpot with a generous 1 gallon (4 L) water to a boil over medium-high heat. Add the cleaned chicken, taking care that it fits in the pot without the boiling water overflowing. Add the ginger, shallots, and star anise. Simmer on low for 1 hour.

When the chicken is cooked through, use tongs to lift the chicken out of the pot and submerge it in an ice bath. (Tip: You can test the chicken's doneness by piercing the flesh with a chopstick. If the juices run clear, the chicken is done. If the juices run pink, it isn't.)

Once cool enough to handle, carve the chicken into eight pieces and slice the meat into thin strips or shred it. Return all the chicken bones to the cooking liquid in the pot and add the coriander seeds. Simmer for 30 minutes on low.

Remove and discard all the solids from the stockpot. Stir in 2 tablespoons salt, chicken bouillon, rock sugar, MSG, and fish sauce. Taste and add additional seasonings if you like (keep in mind once the noodles are added, the flavors will mellow).

Assemble and serve:

If using dried noodles: Use a noodle strainer basket to soak for 30 minutes in warm water or 1 hour in cold water. Add the soaked noodles to a 3-quart (3-L) pot of boiling water and cook for 15 to 20 minutes, according to package instructions. Drain and then rinse the noodles under cold water; leave in a noodle strainer basket until ready to portion into bowls.

If using fresh noodles: Each bowl of noodles is prepared individually. For each bowl, measure out 4 to 5 ounces (115 to 140 g) noodles. In a 3-quart (3-L) pot filled with about 2 quarts (2 L) boiling water, cook them in batches for about 20 seconds, until just al dente, then place them in a bowl.

Add a handful of cooked rice noodles and a handful of chicken (strips or shredded) to each bowl. Ladle about 2 cups (480 ml) into each bowl, being sure to submerge the noodles and chicken, then top with white or yellow onion, green onion, cilantro, fried shallots, and a pinch of pepper.

On a separate plate, arrange the bean sprouts, lime wedges, chiles, and Thai basil (the leaves can be ripped off the stem and added directly into the broth as each person desires). Serve with hoisin sauce and Sriracha on the side, so you can add based on personal preference. (Tip: My favorite way to use these condiments is to squeeze both sauces into one ramekin and then dip the meat into it. I squeeze my lime directly into the broth.)

There's a friendly noodle soup rivalry between phở, Vietnam's national dish, and bún bò Huế, the pride of Huế, the former imperial capital of Vietnam and seat of its royal court. In recent years–and at our restaurant–bún bò Huế has become very popular, giving phở a run for its money. The use of lemongrass and chili oil in the stock is specific to its origin in Central Vietnam, a highland region home to an abundance of spices. For the stock in this recipe, you will smash stalks of lemongrass. For the sate sauce, you can mince stalks of lemongrass or buy it pre-minced.

My extra-spicy version is inspired by my auntie, the iconic Vietnamese singer Lynda Trang Dai. Her family happens to be from Huế, and she calls herself the "queen of bún bò Huế," as it's her signature dish to make for friends and family (we love it). When you make the dish, you'll notice its bright red color, which comes from a sate sauce specifically made for bún bò Huế with shrimp paste, soup base mix, and a specific Chiu Chow seasoning powder–which is easy to order online, if you can't find it in your local Asian market. The stock can be frozen for up to 1 month, or refrigerated for 3 to 4 days, if you want to make it in advance and reheat it just before serving.

Central Vietnamese Lemongrass Beef Soup
Bún Bò Huế

Serves 10 to 12

Ingredients

FOR THE STOCK:

6 pounds (2.7 kg) beef bones

1 pound (455 g) lemongrass (about 8 stalks)

4 pounds (1.8 kg) beef shank

6 shallots

3 medium yellow onions

6 ounces (170 g) fresh ginger

1 pineapple, top and skin removed, then halved

FOR THE SATE SAUCE:

½ cup (120 ml) vegetable oil

½ cup (120 g) minced garlic

1 pound (455 g) lemongrass, tough parts removed, flesh minced (about 8 stalks)

2 (16-ounce/455-g) jars spicy beef flavor paste, such as Por Kwan

2 (7-ounce/205-g) cans chili oil, such as Chiu Chow

½ cup (120 ml) fish sauce, such as Three Crabs

3 tablespoons chicken bouillon, such as Totole Granulated Chicken Soup Base Mix

3 tablespoons kosher salt

5 tablespoons (75 g) shrimp paste

1 (2-ounce/55-g) bag Pyramide Gia Vi Bún Bò Huế powder

1 cup (220 g) rock sugar

FOR SERVING:

2 (14-ounce/400-g) bags bún (dried rice vermicelli noodles), such as Bamboo Tree

1 pound (455 g) chả lụa (Vietnamese ham, which can be purchased at any Asian market), thinly sliced

1 bunch cilantro, leaves and stems chopped

1 bunch green onions, chopped

½ head white cabbage, thinly sliced

½ head purple cabbage, thinly sliced

2 pounds (910 g) mung bean sprouts

recipe continued

Method

Make the stock: Preheat the oven to 475°F (245°C). Spread out the beef bones on a sheet pan and roast them for 20 minutes, flipping them halfway through.

In a large stockpot, add 3 gallons (11 L) water and bring to a boil. Add the roasted bones to the boiling water (making sure they are submerged). Use a mallet to smash open the lemongrass stalks. Add the smashed lemongrass, beef shank, shallots, onions, ginger, and pineapple to the pot and simmer for about 45 minutes, then turn down the heat to medium-low and cook for 3 hours. Turn off the heat and remove and discard the pineapple and bones; set aside the beef shank in the refrigerator.

Make the sate sauce: In a wok, bring the oil to medium heat. Add the garlic and minced lemongrass and cook for 3 to 4 minutes until fragrant. Add the spicy beef paste, chili oil, fish sauce, chicken bouillon, salt, shrimp paste, and Pyramide Gia Vi Bún Bò Huế powder. Bring to high heat and cook for 3 to 4 minutes, stirring occasionally, until fragrant.

Pour the sate sauce into the stock, bring the stock to medium heat, add the rock sugar, and cook for 1 hour at a medium-low simmer.

Assemble and serve: Boil the vermicelli noodles according to the package instructions until al dente, about 10 minutes. Meanwhile, thinly slice the beef shank.

Add a handful of cooked noodles, about 6 slices of beef shank, and 4 slices of chả lụa to each bowl. Ladle 2 cups (480 ml) of the hot stock into each bowl and garnish with cilantro, green onions, both cabbages, and bean sprouts.

Many cities in Vietnam have their own signature dish, or at least their own version of a beloved dish; this noodle soup comes from my mom's hometown of Mỹ Tho, a small city in the Mekong Delta region of Vietnam. In contrast to phở and Central Vietnamese Lemongrass Beef Soup (page 135), it's made with a clear pork stock that's clean and light, with a subtle sweetness from the rock sugar and daikon, yet hearty at the same time thanks in part to the quail eggs. The dish doesn't get as much credit as it deserves, so we sometimes offer it as an off-the-menu special. It's also very versatile: Depending on your mood, you can serve the noodles dry with a bowl of stock on the side, as shown here, or as a regular noodle soup with the noodles and stock served together.

My Tho Noodle Soup
Hủ Tiếu Mỹ Tho
Serves 10 to 12

Ingredients

FOR THE CHAR SIU:
1½ pounds (680 g) pork butt (boneless pork shoulder)

1 (2½-ounce/70-g) bag Chinese barbecue char siu seasoning mix, such as NOH

2 tablespoons kosher salt

2 tablespoons five-spice powder

1 tablespoon hoisin sauce

2 tablespoons honey

FOR THE STOCK:
7 pounds (3.2 kg) pork bones

Kosher salt

1 white onion

1 (2-inch/5-cm) piece fresh ginger, not peeled

8 ounces (225 g) dried shrimp

3 pounds (1.4 kg) white daikon, peeled and halved lengthwise

1 tablespoon kosher salt, or to taste

3 tablespoons fish sauce, such as Three Crabs

2½ tablespoons rock sugar, or to taste

1 tablespoon chicken bouillon, such as Totole Granulated Chicken Soup Base Mix

FOR THE GARNISHES:
18 quail eggs

1 pound (455 g) ground pork

1 pound (455 g) jumbo shrimp (about 16 to 20), peeled and deveined

FOR ASSEMBLY AND SERVING:
3 (14-ounce/400-g) bags dried hủ tiếu (rice) noodles, such as Nam Vang Tapioca Noodles

1 bunch green onions, chopped

1 pound (455 g) mung bean sprouts

1 bunch Chinese chives, chopped

1 bunch cilantro, leaves and stems chopped

1 cup (105 g) Crispy Fried Garlic (page 63)

2 (6-ounce/170-g) bags fried fish balls, such as Shung Kee Food

5 to 6 red Thai chiles, sliced on the bias

Freshly ground black pepper

recipe continued

Method

Season the char siu: Place the pork butt on a sheet pan and, wearing gloves, use your hands to rub it evenly with salt, char siu seasoning, and five-spice powder until the meat is completely coated. Place the sheet pan in the refrigerator, covered, for a minimum of 4 hours (or overnight for maximum flavor) to marinate, until the pork takes on a hot-pink color from the spices.

Make the stock: Wash and salt the bones and set aside for 15 minutes, which will help reduce any odor while cooking. Bring a medium pot of water to a boil, add the salted bones, and cook for 15 to 20 minutes, until the scum and impurities rise to the top. Turn off the heat, remove the bones from the pot, rinse them in cold water, and set aside. Discard the cooking water.

In a 12-quart (12-L) stockpot, bring 2 gallons (8 L) water to a boil on medium-high heat. Cut the white onion in half and char the halves by holding them with tongs over the burner on your stovetop for about 3 minutes per side (or put them on a tray under the broiler to char for about 4 minutes), until fragrant. Likewise, char the piece of ginger for about 3 minutes on each side until fragrant (or 4 minutes if using a broiler). Add the charred onion and the bones to the stock. Smash the ginger with a mallet, then rinse off the charred skin, and add the ginger to the stock.

In a 12-inch (30-cm) frying pan, toast the dried shrimp over medium heat for 5 minutes, which will help to draw out their flavor. Add the toasted shrimp to the stock along with the daikon. Cook for 1½ hours over medium heat, ensuring the stock is a light yellow color. Continue cooking the stock over medium heat for an additional 1½ hours.

Use a spider to remove and discard the bones, onions, daikon, and ginger from the stock. Strain the stock through a cheesecloth or fine-mesh strainer. Add the salt, fish sauce, rock sugar, and chicken bouillon. Simmer for 15 minutes. Taste to check the seasoning, and add more salt or rock sugar based on preference of saltiness or sweetness, respectively.

Cook the char siu: Take the sheet pan containing the seasoned char siu out of the refrigerator. Preheat the oven to 350°F (175°C). Remove the covering and place the sheet pan in the oven. Bake it for 2 hours. In a small saucepan, boil ½ cup (120 ml) water and add the hoisin sauce and honey to make a glaze. Stir to incorporate, then remove from the heat. Every 30 minutes, take a brush and glaze the char siu evenly while it is in the oven. After 2 hours, turn off the oven. Let the pork sit for 15 minutes and then remove it from the oven to let it cool. Slice the pork into 1- to 2-inch (2.5- to 5-cm) slices, without removing any fat from the meat.

Prepare the garnishes: Meanwhile, add enough water to a 2- to 3-quart (2- to 3-L) saucepot to fill the pot halfway, then bring the water to a boil. Add the quail eggs and boil for 3 minutes, or until hard. Remove them, set aside, and peel when cool. In the same pot, dump out the cooking water used to boil the quail eggs and boil 4 cups (1 L) water and poach the ground pork for 5 to 7 minutes, using a wooden spoon to break it apart. Don't worry about overcooking it. Once cooked, drain and set the poached ground pork aside.

In the same pot, bring 4 cups (1 L) water to a boil and poach the jumbo shrimp for 1 to 2 minutes, until pink and cooked through. Drain the shrimp and set aside.

Assemble and serve: Boil the rice noodles and fish balls according to the package instructions. In each serving bowl, add a handful of noodles and some of the sliced char siu pork, quail egg, shrimp, ground pork, green onions, bean sprouts, chives, cilantro, crispy garlic, 1 to 2 fish balls, and red Thai chiles, if desired. Finish each bowl with a pinch of ground black pepper. You can either top your bowl with hot stock and serve as a noodle soup or serve the broth on the side, garnished with green onion and chives.

Tết Noodles

Serves 6 to 8

Growing up, my family used to visit Los Angeles often. When I was a kid, we discovered a Beverly Hills restaurant called Crustacean, which is famous for its garlic crab and noodles. Every time we visited LA, I would ask to go back to Crustacean for this favorite. Our rich and creamy Tết noodle recipe is my reinterpretation of that iconic dish. We originally released it as a limited-time special around Lunar New Year, or Tết, but our customers were furious when we took it off the menu, so we kept it. It's not really a traditional Vietnamese dish, but it's definitely a Madame Vo staple. We love carbs.

Ingredients

FOR THE SAUCE:

2 tablespoons tomato paste

1 cup (240 ml) heavy cream

2 tablespoons fish sauce, such as Three Crabs

5 tablespoons (75 g) sugar

Kosher salt and ground black pepper

1 (16-ounce/455-g) bag dried lo mein egg noodles, such as Twin Marquis

3 tablespoons vegetable oil, for frying

8 tiger prawns, peeled and deveined

¼ cup (½ stick / 55 g) unsalted butter

1 tablespoon minced garlic

8 ounces (225 g) lump crabmeat

¼ cup (26 g) Crispy Fried Garlic (page 63)

1 green onion, sliced

½ bunch cilantro, leaves and stems chopped

Method

In a small bowl, combine the tomato paste and heavy cream and whisk until silky smooth and orange. Add the fish sauce, sugar, and a pinch each of salt and pepper. Stir the sauce together until the ingredients are evenly mixed and set aside.

Fill a medium stockpot with water and bring to a boil. Add the lo mein noodles and cook for 5 minutes, or according to package instructions; strain and set aside.

In a large frying pan, heat the oil on high heat and pan-sear the prawns on both sides for 2 minutes, or until they turn bright pink and start to brown. Remove the prawns and set aside on a plate. Wipe the frying pan clean with a paper towel and bring it back to high heat.

In the same pan, add the butter and swirl to evenly coat the pan with the melted butter. Add the minced garlic and fry with the butter for 30 to 40 seconds. Next, add the cooked lo mein noodles and toss to evenly coat with the butter. Add the tomato cream sauce and toss to evenly coat. Add the cooked prawns and the crabmeat to the pan and toss for 1 minute to distribute and warm them.

Serve the noodles immediately, topped with the fried garlic, green onions, and cilantro.

This is Madame Vo's take on a Chinese-Cambodian stir-fried hủ tiếu noodle dish that my dad taught me to make. However, rather than use tapioca noodles, our version is made with regular dried rice stick noodles, or bánh phở, the same shape as you'll see in phở or pad Thai. It's a simple recipe that works perfectly for weeknight dinners. Besides garlic, a key ingredient here is the Golden Mountain seasoning sauce, which is a staple of Southeast Asian kitchens (see page 34). Made from fermented soybeans, this sauce adds a hit of umami.

Garlic Noodles
Bánh Phở Xào Tỏi

Serves 4 to 6

Method

Fill a medium stockpot with water and bring to a boil. Add the noodles and cook until softened but still retain some bite, about 6 minutes. Drain the noodles in a colander, rinse with cold water, and set aside to dry until ready to use.

In a large nonstick wok, heat 1½ tablespoons of the oil on high. Add the whisked eggs and cook, stirring occasionally, until they reach a medium-runny consistency. Remove from the pan and set aside on a plate.

Heat another 1½ tablespoons oil in the wok. Pan-sear the shrimp for 1 to 2 minutes, until golden brown. Remove and set aside on a plate.

Add ¼ cup (60 ml) oil, then add the garlic and cook until golden brown. Add the reserved noodles and stir evenly on high heat to incorporate. Add the dark soy sauce, seasoning sauce, sugar, MSG, and black pepper and continue to toss to ensure the noodles are evenly coated in seasoning.

After the noodles are completely brown in color, about another 2 to 3 minutes, add the reserved scrambled eggs, shrimp, and green onions. Toss evenly for about 2 minutes to incorporate. Sprinkle with the white pepper and serve immediately.

Ingredients

½ (1-pound/455-g) bag bánh phở (dried rice stick noodles), such as Erawan Oriental Style Rice Noodles (use either medium width or wide noodles)

Vegetable oil, for frying

4 large eggs, whisked

10 ounces (280 g) shrimp, peeled (leave tail part of shell on, if you like)

10 cloves garlic, minced (about ¼ cup / 40 g)

½ tablespoon dark soy sauce

1½ tablespoons Golden Mountain seasoning sauce

¼ cup (50 g) sugar

½ teaspoon monosodium glutamate (MSG)

½ teaspoon ground black pepper

1 green onion, sliced in half lengthwise, then chopped into 1-inch-long (2.5-cm) pieces

½ teaspoon ground white pepper

Seafood Crispy Noodles with Gravy
Mì Xào Giòn Hải Sản

Serves 4 to 6

This festive dish—often served family-style at parties and gatherings—combines fried chow mein noodles with a thick, savory gravy-like sauce. The noodles are crispy until softened by the gravy, which is poured on top when the dish hits the table. The result is a mix of soft, chewy, and crunchy noodles, depending on how much gravy soaks in. It's the combination of these contrasting textures that makes the perfect bite. The dish is Chinese influenced, but the Vietnamese version tends to be a bit sweeter.

Ingredients

Vegetable oil, for frying

3 tablespoons minced garlic

8 ounces (225 g) sea scallops (about 8 pieces)

8 ounces (225 g) tiger prawns (around 5), peeled

1 bag (16-ounce/455-g) fish balls or cakes, such as Best Fried Fish Balls

¼ cup (20 to 25 g) julienned carrots

1 (8-ounce/230-g) can baby corn, such as Aroy-D

8 ounces (225 g) baby bok choy, quartered

8 ounces (225 g) cauliflower, chopped into florets

1 cup (240 ml) chicken stock

¼ cup (60 ml) fish sauce, such as Three Crabs

¼ cup (60 ml) distilled white vinegar

1 tablespoon chicken bouillon, such as Totole Granulated Chicken Soup Base Mix

¾ cup (100 g) sugar

3 tablespoons ground black pepper

1 teaspoon monosodium glutamate (MSG)

3 tablespoons cornstarch

1 (16-ounce/450-g) bag refrigerated and dried chow mein egg noodles, such as Twin Marquis

2 green onions, julienned

2 red Thai chiles, sliced thin

Method

Heat a 12-inch (30-cm) nonstick frying pan on high. Add ¼ cup (60 ml) vegetable oil and the garlic. Cook the garlic for 2 to 3 minutes, until golden brown. Add the scallops, tiger prawns, and fish balls and cook for 5 minutes, or until lightly browned. Add the carrots, baby corn, baby bok choy, and cauliflower and stir until combined. Add the chicken stock, fish sauce, vinegar, chicken bouillon, and ½ cup (120 ml) water. Bring to boil for 4 minutes. Add the sugar, pepper, and MSG and stir until combined.

In a small bowl, mix the cornstarch with ¼ cup (60 ml) warm water to create a slurry. Stir the cornstarch slurry into the prawn-and-vegetable mixture and cook for 3 to 4 minutes, or until the gravy thickens, then set aside to cool.

Preheat 12-inch (30-cm) frying pan on high heat and fill the pan halfway with oil. Once the oil is bubbling, place the chow mein noodles into the hot oil and deep-fry them for 3 to 5 minutes, until they crisp up and form one connected piece. Remove the noodles with a slotted spoon and place on a paper towel to drain off the oil.

Once you are ready to serve, place the noodles on a large plate. Top the fried noodles with the gravy and serve hot, garnished with green onions and red Thai chiles.

Lemongrass Beef Vermicelli
Bún Bò Xào

Serves 4 to 6

Xào refers to stir-frying in Vietnamese cuisine. Featuring beef stir-fried in lemongrass, this dish is essentially a beef noodle salad, since the noodles can be enjoyed at room temperature with the meat on top. Served with cucumber, mint, and basil, it's light, refreshing, and healthy—ideal for hot summer days.

Method

Make the noodles: Boil the vermicelli noodles, until al dente per the package instructions, about 7 to 8 minutes. Rinse the noodles with cold water and set aside to cool.

Make the beef: Add the vegetable oil to a 12-inch (30-cm) frying pan and bring the oil to high heat. Add the garlic, lemongrass, and shallots and cook for 2 to 3 minutes, stirring often, until fragrant. Add half the sliced beef and stir-fry for 2 minutes, making sure the pan is not overcrowded. Remove and stir-fry the other half of the sliced beef. Return the remaining beef to the pan and add the fish sauce, chili sauce, sugar, oyster sauce, and ground black pepper. Squeeze in the juice of ½ lime. Cook for 3 to 4 minutes until the sauce reduces (tip: you should have just enough to slightly glaze the beef).

Make the simple green onion oil: In a 2-quart (2-L) saucepan, heat the vegetable oil to high then add the green onions. Stir for 1 minute and then turn off heat.

Assemble the noodle salad: Add a handful of bean sprouts and lettuce leaves to each bowl, then top with a handful of the cooled vermicelli noodles. Add 8 to 10 slices of the beef to each bowl and top with cucumber, basil, mint, crispy shallots, red onion, pickled vegetables, and a drizzle of the green onion oil. Serve the Vietnamese dipping sauce as a dressing in small bowls or ramekins on the side. Squeeze ½ lime into the dipping sauce or over the dish for a little extra acidity, if desired.

Ingredients

FOR THE NOODLES:
1 (14-ounce/400-g) bag dried rice vermicelli noodles (bag bún), such as Bamboo Tree

FOR THE BEEF:
½ cup (120 ml) vegetable oil, for frying

½ cup (120 g) minced garlic

½ cup (25 to 30 g) minced lemongrass

2 shallots, thinly sliced

2 pounds (910 g) beef tenderloin, thinly sliced and patted dry with a paper towel

¼ cup (60 ml) fish sauce, such as Three Crabs

1 tablespoon chili sauce, such as Huy Fong Chili Garlic Sauce

¼ cup (50 g) sugar

1 tablespoon oyster sauce, such as Lee Kum Kee

1 teaspoon ground black pepper

½ lime

FOR THE SIMPLE GREEN ONION OIL:
½ cup (120 ml) vegetable oil

1 bunch green onions, chopped

FOR THE NOODLE SALAD:
8 ounces (225 g) mung bean sprouts

1 head leaf lettuce

4 to 6 mini cucumbers, thinly sliced

1 bunch fresh basil, stems removed

1 bunch fresh mint, stems removed

Crispy Fried Shallots (page 61)

1 red onion, sliced

½ cup (60 to 80 g) Pickled Vegetables (page 45)

Vietnamese Dipping Sauce (page 46), for serving

½ lime (optional)

. RICE .

Mama Ly's Fried Rice

Cơm Chiên Mama Ly

Serves 6 to 8

A lot of families have a signature fried rice recipe, but in my house, we have two—one for each of my parents. My dad's take on fried rice is a classic Chinese-style fried rice, flavored with Maggi seasoning and finished off with chopped Chinese sausage (lap cheong in Chinese, and lạp xưởng in Vietnamese). It's a quick-and-easy dish and one of my favorites that he made for me growing up. My mom, never one to turn away from a bit of healthy competition, wanted to make her own fried rice recipe. She noticed that I loved the tomato-seasoned rice at Vietnamese restaurants, so she created a fried version that offered the same flavor—seasoned with salt, salted butter, and tomato paste. I love both equally, of course, but we serve Mama Ly's at Madame Vo.

Ingredients

⅓ cup (75 ml) tomato paste

2 tablespoons salted butter

½ cup (70 g) chopped boneless chicken breast or thigh

½ cup (65 g) peeled and chopped colossal shrimp (31 to 40)

¼ cup (60 ml) vegetable oil, for frying

½ cup (120 g) minced garlic

2 shallots, finely chopped

½ (16-ounce/455-g) bag frozen peas and carrots

6 cups (775 g) white jasmine rice, cooked, cooled, and refrigerated overnight

¼ cup (50 g) sugar

Kosher salt and ground black pepper

1 tablespoon monosodium glutamate (MSG)

2 green onions, sliced

¼ bunch cilantro, leaves and stems chopped

Method

In a small mixing bowl, whisk the tomato paste with ½ cup (120 ml) water and set aside.

In a medium frying pan over high heat, add the salted butter and lower the heat to medium, to avoid burning the butter. Add the chicken and cook for 5 minutes, stirring occasionally for even cooking. Then add the shrimp and cook for an additional 3 minutes, stirring to combine, until the chicken is cooked through and the shrimp has turned slightly pink and white. Set the butter-coated chicken and shrimp aside.

Lightly clean the frying pan by wiping with a clean paper towel or damp kitchen towel and return the pan to high heat. Add the oil and allow to heat for 30 seconds, then add the garlic and shallots. Cook until aromatic, about 45 seconds. Then add the peas and carrots and cook until lightly browned, about 2 minutes. Add the rice and stir to coat evenly.

Add the tomato paste and water mixture, stirring until the rice takes on an even, light red-orange color. Add the chicken and shrimp, sugar, salt and pepper to taste, and MSG. Stir to evenly combine and cook for about 5 minutes, until the fried rice mixture is slightly browned yet still retains some of the orange color from the tomato paste. Top with the green onions and cilantro and serve.

Various rice and grains for sale at a market in Saigon

Papa Ly's Fried Rice
Cơm Chiên Papa Ly

Serves 6 to 8

Ingredients

1 cup (240 ml) vegetable oil, for frying

3 large eggs, whisked

2 cups (400 g) chopped Chinese sausage, such as Kam Yen Jan

¼ cup (60 g) minced garlic

6 cups (775 g) white jasmine rice, cooked, cooled, and refrigerated overnight

3 tablespoons Maggi seasoning

2 teaspoons monosodium glutamate (MSG)

2 teaspoons ground black pepper

1 tablespoon sugar

2 green onions, sliced

¼ bunch cilantro, leaves and stems chopped

Method

In a medium frying pan, add the oil and bring to high heat. Cook the whisked eggs lightly while stirring, until somewhat still runny, about 3 minutes, and set the eggs aside.

In the same pan, fry the Chinese sausage for 2 minutes and set the sausage aside.

Add the garlic to the pan and fry for about 2 minutes, until lightly brown. Stir in the rice until the garlic is evenly distributed and let the rice fry for at least 3 minutes, or until you hear a faint sizzle.

Add the Maggi seasoning, MSG, pepper, and sugar and stir to thoroughly combine with the rice. Add the reserved scrambled eggs and fried sausage, give the fried rice a final stir to evenly combine the ingredients, and cook until the rice is slightly browned, about 5 minutes. Top with the green onions and cilantro and serve.

TIP FOR PERFECT FRIED RICE
For the best results when making fried rice, always use day-old rice. It takes a bit of extra planning, but this slightly aged rice delivers a much snappier, crispier texture when fried. Freshly steamed white rice, by contrast, retains more moisture, which can affect how crispy the fried rice is.

Papa Ly's Fried Rice (left) and
Mama Ly's Fried Rice (right)

Marinated Chicken Over Rice
Cơm Gà Rô Ti

Serves 6 to 8

Chicken over rice might be the world's most universal dish, and Vietnamese people have made an art of this unpretentious, elemental food. In our recipe, adapted from the version my parents served at their Chinatown restaurant, Paris Sandwich, the marinade for the chicken uses sugar and soy sauce, which caramelizes to make a delicious sauce, perfect for soaking up with rice. Though it's great on its own or with just a bit of fish sauce, you can also serve it with our Tamarind Sauce (page 48).

Ingredients

3 pounds (1.4 kg) skin-on chicken thighs (can be bone-in or boneless)

¾ cup (150 g) sugar

½ cup (120 g) minced garlic

⅓ cup (45 g) minced shallots

1 tablespoon ground white pepper

2 tablespoons five-spice powder

1 tablespoon monosodium glutamate (MSG)

1 tablespoon onion powder

2 tablespoons sesame oil

½ cup (120 ml) soy sauce, such as Mountain Soy Sauce

1 tablespoon dark soy sauce, such as Pearl River Bridge

¼ cup (60 ml) vegetable oil, for frying

FOR SERVING:
6 to 8 cups (775 g to 1 kg) steamed white jasmine rice

Method

Pat the chicken thighs dry with a paper towel and set aside.

In a large bowl, combine ½ cup (120 ml) water with the sugar, garlic, shallots, white pepper, MSG, five-spice powder, onion powder, sesame oil, and both soy sauces. Mix until the sugar dissolves. Add the chicken to the marinade, cover in plastic wrap, and refrigerate for at least 2 hours or, for best flavor, overnight.

In a 12-inch (30-cm) frying pan, add the vegetable oil and bring to high heat. Remove the chicken from the marinade, reserving the marinade sauce, and pan sear the chicken until cooked through, about 5 minutes on each side. Alternatively, the chicken can be grilled on a gas-powered grill for 8 to 10 minutes on each side.

In a 2-quart (2-L) saucepan, bring the reserved marinade to a boil over high heat.

Serve the chicken over the steamed rice (about 1 cup / 130 g per serving), topped with the hot marinade sauce and garnished with pickled vegetables, cucumber, and herbs.

OPENING MADAME VO

The Trials and Tribulations of Running a Restaurant

The night we opened, Yen and I were both nervous. After months of seeing the space come to life, it was showtime. Everything was on the line. We had no idea if anyone would come, but we banked on the fact that people in NYC were dying for a modern Vietnamese restaurant. We didn't even know what PR was. All we had was an Instagram handle and $50,000 in the hole. We needed revenue badly.

To our genuine surprise, people just showed up. That night, we did no more than forty covers, pocketed nine hundred dollars and change, and were totally wiped out. It was me, a sous chef, and a prep cook in the kitchen. I remember our dishwashing machine hadn't even been installed yet, so the prep cook spent the night washing dishes by hand. Our front-of-house was two servers plus Yen hosting, bartending, and ringing up payments. By the time we closed the doors after the last customer, we couldn't feel our legs.

These are the kind of memories we wanted to revisit with this book. We were so young, and so inexperienced. It was the first time turning on the car engine, and it felt like we were figuring out everything while in motion. I remember our signature bò lúc lắc dish (sizzling beef cubes on a skillet) only really came together for the first time when a customer ordered it.

This was a dish we had really wanted to nail, because we knew the aroma and smoke would get the dining room excited. I had been working on the recipe for weeks with no luck—every marinade we tried came out salty—so when the ticket came in, I just wok-seared some unmarinated beef with Maggi seasoning, sugar, garlic, butter, and green onion and sent it out. We all held our breath when Yen approached the customer to ask if they liked it, and they did. We haven't changed the recipe since.

Most of the rest of the menu came from our parents—things Yen and I both grew up eating. I wanted to show them I could do their recipes, my way. Our now-famous Madame Phở (page 129) was my mom's recipe, with the addition of a big bone-in short rib, which Yen's mom used to give her because she loved meat so much. The Chicken Curry (page 111) came from my dad, while the Salt and Pepper Calamari (page 91) was from my mom, and the wings (page 74) were from Yen's dad.

The first few months after we opened were grueling. Day in and day out, Yen and I opened and closed the restaurant. By the time we got home, we would be too tired to do anything, knowing we would need to be back up at six the next morning. A couple of weeks in, the crowd we got on opening night dwindled, except for some day-one regulars.

It was all a blur, but I remember at one point sitting at the last table in the restaurant, head in my hands, just crying. Yen had told me, "Honey, we can only keep going on like this for three months before we have to close the restaurant." My parents would come to visit at lunch, and I would be too depressed to talk to them. At home, I hoped something would change, wondering what it had all been for.

Looking back at this do-or-die moment, we think some of this slowdown had to do with our terrible Yelp reviews, which had left us sitting at three and a half stars. We're not saying our food was perfect back then, but a good majority of the reviews had more to do with our prices. People simply couldn't

fathom that a bowl of phở would cost sixteen dollars. They were so fixated on the perceived value of the food that they would say negative things before they even came to the restaurant. Some would message me on Instagram, saying, "What's wrong with you?"

For some context, let's rewind to the making of the menu. When I opened my restaurant, I knew I didn't want to price Vietnamese food cheaply. The older generation did this out of necessity—they knew they had to offer the best value to compete. I saw what my parents went through. But I ate out a lot. I had eaten fine-dining Chinese food, Thai food, and Korean food—which all have a long history in NYC. Among all those Asian cuisines, Vietnamese food had been relegated to the sidelines as a cuisine that was exclusively "cheap eats."

That really bothered me. I knew we were more than that. I knew what we were worth. And I thought the best way to do justice to the previous generation, who paved the road for Americans to learn about Vietnamese food, was to ensure that Vietnamese food was priced accurately going forward. That also meant it had to be fair to customers. The price had to match the quality. So, for our bò lúc lắc, I used Angus rib eye instead of the usual sirloin. Where others would use baby shrimp, I used extra-large jumbo shrimp or tiger prawn. In broths, I upgraded regular bones to neck and leg bones.

When we realized the clock was ticking and we had three months left to go, we decided we were going to go out with a bang. At the time, our phở was getting noticed on social media because the bone-in short rib made it look so dramatic in photos. So we started inviting in influencers one at a time to try it. One post at a time, a different, more accepting food-focused clientele slowly started coming to Madame Vo. While we were still really in limbo, people who tried the phở would tell us they loved it. It gave us the hope to keep going.

Our bone-in short rib phở came from real family traditions, so we were a little surprised and deeply honored that it made such an impact on social media—and that this style of short rib phở has become such a phenomenon globally. We're grateful to be able to touch so many Vietnamese people and Vietnamese food lovers on Instagram, and to be part of the movement to showcase the many different sides of this versatile dish.

Our Fairy Godmother

Then came that day in May 2017, and the phone call that changed everything: "Hey, this is Sarah Jessica Parker. Can we get a reservation for two tonight at 7:30?" Yen ran into the kitchen freaking out. I started freaking out too. The reservation time came and went, and no one showed up. Then, after what felt like the longest seventeen minutes ever, she came in at 7:47 p.m. on the dot and apologized for being late. Yen runs back in to tell me, and I start instructing our staff: Everything needs to be perfect for this table.

At this point, I was so tired. The previous few months had beat me down hard. I knew I looked like I was about to bawl my eyes out. But as she was eating and having a good time, I decided to come out in my chef coat to introduce myself and just say, "Hey, it's such an honor to meet you. We're big fans and it means a lot that you're eating at our restaurant." I asked her how the meal was, and she told us she was impressed, and that she had never had anything like this before.

More relieved than anything else, I offered to comp her meal. I'll never forget: She grabbed my hand and said, "Listen, the food was good. But if you comp my meal, I am never coming back here again. I just want to support you guys."

We were thrilled about getting a visit from SJP, but we didn't really think much of it. We just hoped she would tell her friends about it. But 30 minutes after she left the restaurant, my phone started blowing

up. Sarah had posted a photo of the front of Madame Vo to her Instagram feed, with the caption:

For anyone wondering where to eat in our fair city for locals or visitors put @madamevonyc at the top of your list. I've been waiting for months, expectations were high and I'm already plotting my return. East 10th St on the land of Manhattan. x, SJ

I looked up from my phone at Yen and I said, "We just got one thousand followers." The next morning, we showed up to work like any other day. But when we turned the corner to Tenth Street, we saw a huge line going from the very middle of the block, where Madame Vo sits, all the way to the Chase Bank on the corner of Second Avenue.

We opened at noon and customers started pouring in. By the time we closed at 3:30 p.m., I had to run to the supermarket to buy more meat and short rib. At 5:30 p.m., the dinner service was equally packed. I don't know if Sarah remembers it as vividly, but this day changed our lives. I was truly flabbergasted. And this is why, to this day, we refer to Sarah Jessica Parker as our má nuôi, which in Vietnamese translates to "second mother" or "godmother."

On Vietnamese Celebrations

Food is central to celebrations in every culture, but for Vietnamese people, it often carries a greater symbolic meaning. The largest celebration in Vietnamese culture is **Lunar New Year**, or Tết, typically celebrated in late January or early February. During this time, the whole country shuts down for nearly two weeks as people travel home to celebrate "an Tết" (literally: eat Tết) with their families.

For Tết, we enjoy dishes like bánh chưng, or sticky rice cakes wrapped in banana leaves, that represent the earth, sky, and our departed ancestors. We also eat noodles, which symbolize longevity, and a whole fish, which symbolizes abundance. Meanwhile, garnishes like pickled vegetables are eaten to help cleanse the body and reset it ahead of the new year.

Other major festivals in Vietnam include the **Mid-Autumn Festival**, or Tết Trung Thu, which typically falls in September or October. Some of the foods for this holiday include the iconic mooncakes filled with lotus seed paste or red bean paste, which represent family and unity. Fruit trays are popular for all Vietnamese festivals, as they symbolize prosperity and are often offered at the altar of ancestors.

And if you ever attend a Vietnamese wedding or other family celebration, you might encounter bò bảy món, or beef seven ways, which, as the name suggests, is a traditional seven-course menu of beef dishes. This is perhaps for a later cookbook, but we did include our favorite item that's typically included in the list: bò lá lốt—beef wrapped in betel leaf (page 95).

Pro-tip: If you're showing up to a Vietnamese party, bring a bottle of nice whiskey or cognac, especially brands like Hennessy, Remy Martin, or Martell. Cognac in particular carries significance for Vietnamese people, as it's a French product and, during colonial times, was seen as a status symbol. Your hosts will thank you!

Defining Vietnamese Nhậu Culture

Beyond holidays, Vietnamese people love to celebrate on a regular basis, which is the foundation of Vietnamese nhậu culture. To "ăn nhậu" literally means to "eat and drink," but it's more than that. In this style of gastropub culture, similar to a Japanese izakaya, it's common to get together over grilled foods and snackable seafood like snails, eaten over hours with plentiful beer on the side. It means to eat and drink—for no reason at all.

This was the inspiration for our second restaurant, Monsieur Vo, which is an ode to our fathers and the men in our lives—who we grew up seeing indulging in the art of nhậu. While the restaurant is less focused on seafood and is more focused on grilled meats, we still try to capture the idea that the Vietnamese sense of community is all about coming together over food and drink.

On the Magic of Nướng, the Art of Vietnamese Barbecue

Walking around the streets in Vietnam, it's more common than not to catch a whiff of marinated, grilled meat cooking on open flames. At Vietnamese get-togethers in the States, it's common to see folks grilling too—like they would at an American barbecue on the Fourth of July. This traditional style of Vietnamese barbecuing, called "nướng," is a popular cooking technique that can be applied to meat, seafood, and vegetables.

What separates Vietnamese grilling from other forms of barbecue are its marinades, which typically include a mix of lemongrass, star anise, garlic, sugar, and fish sauce. In Vietnam, charcoal-grilling is commonly used to activate the aromatics, caramelizing the sugar and fish sauce. But that same marinade can be used to cook on a gas grill, or even in a frying pan, so these dishes are equally popular inside home kitchens.

Vietnamese barbecue encompasses a wide range of dishes, but generally you can expect to find a marinated meat paired with a starch such as noodles or rice. In fact, Vietnamese nướng dishes are named by their starch and protein. Here are some examples:

- **Ga Nướng Sả**
  is marinated grilled lemongrass chicken. "Ga" means "chicken" and "sả" means "lemongrass." In this case, the chicken is marinated in lemongrass, garlic, fish sauce, and sugar, then grilled until charred.

- **Bún Thịt Nướng**
  (page 165) is rice vermicelli noodles (bún) topped with marinated grilled pork loin (thịt). Note: Thịt can also mean meat in general, but in this dish, it refers to pork loin.

- **Com Suon Nướng**
  (page 167), by contrast, means rice (com) topped with marinated grilled pork chop (suon).

Get it?

One of the best things about Vietnamese barbecue is that a few hours of marinating time can do the trick; after that, the meat or other protein just needs a few minutes on the grill—no smoker or other unusual equipment required. These grilled foods are super quick and easy to cook, so they are perfect for everyday meals, even though nướng-style dishes are often associated with celebrations, as grilling and barbecuing are across cultures. It's both a cooking method as well as a way of life.

All you need to try out nướng is our Grilled Meats Marinade (page 162), which is our all-purpose, lemongrass-dominant Vietnamese barbecue marinade. You can keep this on hand to use for a quick weekday lunch or backyard BBQ with friends.

Beyond the rice and noodle preparation styles mentioned here, you may also serve Vietnamese grilled meats with dry rice paper, or bánh tráng, which can be used to make your own rolls. Follow the same rolling method featured in our Autumn Rolls (page 82) or Spring Rolls (page 84) except with your choice of grilled meats, herbs, and pickled vegetables. This kind of customization is what makes Vietnamese food fun and interactive—ideal for big groups and parties.

Grilled Meats Marinade
Gia Vị Nướng

Makes 2 quarts (2 L)

Our nướng, or grilling, marinade is a reliable, versatile recipe that you can use with your choice of protein. It's made with fragrant star anise as well as lemongrass, which can be purchased pre-minced for this recipe. It's slightly less viscous than a conventional marinade and is meant to submerge the meat fully. We like to use it on pork chops, pork loin, and boneless, skin-on chicken thighs, in particular. See below for some tips to adapt these methods based on your preferred protein. We like to eat the grilled meats with rice, vermicelli, rice paper (see page 94), or as a bánh mì, along with lettuce, pickled daikon and carrot, cucumber, pineapple, mint, basil, Vietnamese coriander, and Thai chile peppers. It's meant to be flexible, interactive, and fun.

Ingredients

1 cup (240 ml) fish sauce, such as Three Crabs

2 cups (225 g) chopped lemongrass (about 8.4 ounces/ 6 stalks)

1 cup (120 g) minced garlic

2 cups (400 g) sugar

10 to 15 whole star anise

¼ cup monosodium glutamate (MSG)

½ cup (120 ml) vegetable oil

Method

In a large bowl, combine the fish sauce, lemongrass, garlic, sugar, star anise, MSG, and oil. Add 2 cups (480 ml) water to the bowl and let the marinade rest at room temperature for at least 30 minutes before using. You can store the marinade in an airtight container in the refrigerator for up to 2 weeks.

TIPS ON HOW TO BARBECUE

This recipe creates enough marinade to marinate 3 to 4 pounds (1.4 to 1.8 kg) meat of your choice.

Slice your preferred meat if desired (e.g., we like to thinly slice pork loin into ½-inch-thick [2-cm] pieces but keep pork chops and chicken thighs whole). Use a paper towel to pat the meat dry.

Add the meat to the large bowl of marinade, cover in plastic wrap, and refrigerate for 2 hours or, for best flavor, overnight.

Heat a grill for 4 minutes on high. Add the marinated protein to the grill, lower the heat to medium, and cook as described in the following recipes. (We use medium heat with this marinade, due to the high sugar content.)

For all proteins, check the meat for doneness with an instant-read thermometer. For instance, for chicken thighs, grill them on medium heat for 12 minutes on each side until they reach 165°F (75°C). The pork loin should reach 145°F (65°C).

While the combinations and possibilities for grilled or nướng (see page 160) dishes are endless, one of our favorite recipes in this category is grilled pork and vermicelli, which might be described as a pork noodle salad, since the noodles can be presented at room temperature with the meat on top. This is Yen's go-to lunchtime dish because it's quick and easy and not too heavy.

· MEAT ·

Grilled Pork Vermicelli
Bún Thịt Nướng

Serves 6

Method

Marinate the pork: Add the pork to the large bowl of marinade, cover in plastic wrap, and refrigerate for 2 hours or, for best flavor, overnight.

Make the noodles: Boil the vermicelli noodles until al dente, according to the package instructions, 7 to 8 minutes. Rinse the noodles with cold water and set aside to cool.

Grill the pork: Heat a gas-powered grill for 4 minutes on high. Add the marinated pork slices to the grill in a single layer, lower the heat to medium, and cook for 6 minutes on each side. Alternatively, add the vegetable oil to a 12-inch (30-cm) frying pan and bring the oil to medium heat. Sear the meat in the oil for about 5 minutes on each side, until cooked through and golden brown. Remove from the heat.

Assemble and serve: Add a handful of bean sprouts and lettuce leaves to each bowl, then top with a handful of vermicelli noodles. Add 5 to 6 slices of meat to each bowl and top with sliced cucumber, basil and mint leaves, crushed peanuts, fried shallots, and a drizzle of green onion oil. Serve with Vietnamese dipping sauce on the side as a dressing.

Ingredients

FOR THE PORK:

2 to 3 pounds (910 g to 1.4 kg) pork loin, sliced into ½-inch-thick (1.25-cm) pieces, dried with a paper towel

1 recipe Grilled Meats Marinade (page 162)

⅓ cup (80 ml) vegetable oil, if frying and not grilling

FOR THE NOODLE SALAD:

1 (14-ounce/400-g) bag dried rice vermicelli noodles (bag bún), such as Bamboo Tree

1 pound (455 g) mung bean sprouts

1 head leaf lettuce, thinly sliced

2 mini cucumbers, thinly sliced crosswise

1 bunch fresh basil, stems removed

1 bunch fresh mint, stems removed

½ cup (70 g) crushed peanuts

½ cup (28 g) Crispy Fried Shallots (page 61) or store-bought fried shallots, such as Wangderm

½ cup (120 ml) Green Onion Oil (page 55)

FOR SERVING:
Vietnamese Dipping Sauce (page 46)

We love this pork and rice dish because it brings together so many of the building blocks found in this cookbook, including our grilling marinade, pickled vegetables, green onion oil, and Vietnamese Dipping Sauce (page 46). These are foundational ingredients we always keep in our kitchen, in case we need to throw together a fast but filling lunch like this. We prefer to use a thin pork chop, as it absorbs our marinade better, and we want the flavors of the marinade to shine. However, you may use a thick-cut pork chop if you desire.

Grilled Pork Chop Over Rice
Cơm Sườn Nướng

Serves 4 to 6

Method

Add the pork chops to a large bowl and add enough marinade until the pork chops are submerged. Cover in plastic wrap and refrigerate for 2 hours or, for best flavor, overnight. Extra marinade may be saved for other recipes or additional pork chops.

Grill the pork: Heat a gas-powered grill for 4 minutes on high. Pat down the marinated pork to prevent splatter, then add it to the grill, lower the heat to medium, and cook for 10 minutes on each side. Alternatively, add the vegetable oil to a 12-inch (30-cm) frying pan and bring the oil to medium heat. Sear the meat for about 5 minutes on each side, until cooked through and golden brown.

Assemble and serve: On each serving plate, arrange 1 cup (129 g) steamed rice, 1 or 2 pork chops, 1 tablespoon pickled veggies, and a couple of sprigs cilantro. Spoon 1 to 2 tablespoons of the green onion oil over the top.

In a medium saucepan over high heat, add a splash of oil and then crack 1 egg into the pan and cook until the egg whites turn opaque and the edges start to brown and become crispy. Remove from the pan with a spatula and repeat for each egg. Top each serving of rice with an egg. Garnish with red chiles, chopped green onions, and cucumbers. Serve the Vietnamese dipping sauce on the side in small bowls or ramekins.

Ingredients

2 to 3 pounds (910 g to 1.4 kg) pork chops (6 to 8 chops), sliced ½-inch (1.25-cm) thick by your butcher

½ recipe Grilled Meats Marinade (page 162)

¼ cup (60 ml) vegetable oil, if not grilling, plus more for cooking the eggs

6 cups (775 g) steamed white jasmine rice

½ cup (80 g) Pickled Vegetables (page 45)

½ cup (120 ml) Green Onion Oil (page 55)

Handful fresh cilantro sprigs

4 to 6 large eggs

red Thai chiles, sliced

Green onions, chopped

Cucumbers, sliced into half-moons

Vietnamese Dipping Sauce (page 46), for serving

Lúc lắc means "shaking" or "jiggling," and it refers to the way the cubes of beef sizzle as they hit the piping hot skillet. This is an all-time favorite of Vietnamese kids, including me when I was growing up. We eat it with white rice and an egg, or with Mama Ly's Fried Rice (page 148). Our signature recipe for the beef, which simply includes Maggi, butter, and sugar cooked in a wok, was a serendipitous solution that we figured out on the night we opened Madame Vo. At the restaurant, we heat a cast-iron skillet and then serve the beef in the skillet so that it sizzles and smokes–plus, we crack the egg directly into the skillet. You may present the dish this way at home for some added flair, but it's not necessary. We don't recommend storing this dish as the meat gets tough–and we suspect there won't be leftovers anyway!

Shaking Beef
Bò Lúc Lắc
Serves 4 to 6

Method

Bring a 12-inch (30-cm) frying pan or wok to high heat and add the vegetable oil. Stir-fry the garlic in the oil for 1 to 2 minutes, until fragrant. Reduce the heat to medium-high and add the rib eye cubes and pan-sear for 2 to 3 minutes, tossing to sear on all sides, then add the butter. Add the Maggi seasoning, sugar, pepper, and green onions. Bring the pan to high heat for 3 to 4 minutes until the sauce caramelizes and thickens to a glossy, syrupy consistency that coats the beef; it should not be watery. However, not all of the sauce should cook off completely. There will be about ¼ cup (60 ml) left in the pan.

Serve with the white rice and, if you like, sunny-side up eggs. To serve in a cast-iron skillet, preheat the skillet for 3 minutes on high heat. Add 1 teaspoon of oil on the end of the skillet, crack an egg into the pan, and cook sunny-side up. Add the cooked beef to the skillet and sizzle to serve.

Ingredients

3 tablespoons vegetable oil

6 tablespoons (96 g) minced garlic

1½ pounds (680 g) rib eye, cut in 1½-inch (3.8-cm) cubes

3 tablespoons unsalted butter

⅓ cup (80 ml) Maggi seasoning

¼ cup (50 g) sugar

1 tablespoon ground black pepper

1 cup (55 g) chopped green onion (white parts only)

FOR SERVING:

2 cups (260 g) cooked white jasmine rice

6 sunny-side-up eggs (optional)

Pineapple Spareribs
Sườn Xào Khóm

Serves 4 to 6

This is the first dish that Yen learned to make at home when she went away for college. It's a simple home-style dish that isn't typically served in restaurants. I also grew up eating these pineapple spareribs because my mom loved fruit, and she always thought that pairing fruit with fatty meat would make it more "healthy." You can eat the ribs with a side of steamed white jasmine rice. To keep the dish warm, we sometimes serve the spare ribs in a clay pot, as shown.

Ingredients

1 teaspoon kosher salt

3 pounds (1.4 kg) spareribs, cut into 3-inch (8-cm) pieces

¼ cup (60 ml) vegetable oil

¼ pineapple, cored and cut into 2-inch (5-cm) chunks

¼ cup (60 g) minced garlic

¼ cup (60 ml) oyster sauce, such as Lee Kum Kee

¾ cup (180 ml) fish sauce, such as Three Crabs

3 tablespoons dark soy sauce, such as Pearl River Bridge

¾ cup (150 g) sugar

2 tablespoons ground black pepper

4 green onions, chopped

2 red Thai chile peppers, sliced, for garnish (optional)

Method

Fill a 3-quart (3-L) pot with 2 quarts (2 L) water, add the salt, and bring to a boil. Parboil the spareribs until they are partially cooked and the exterior turns light gray, about 40 minutes. Drain and rinse the ribs under cold running water before setting aside on a large paper towel to dry.

Preheat a 12-inch (30-cm) frying pan or wok with the vegetable oil to high heat. Cook the pineapple in the oil, tossing for 5 minutes, or until golden brown. Add the garlic and cook for 3 minutes, stirring often, or until golden brown. Reduce to low heat. Add the oyster sauce, fish sauce, dark soy sauce, sugar, black pepper, and parboiled spareribs. Stir until combined. Pour in 3 cups (720 ml) water and cook for 15 to 20 minutes, or until the ribs are cooked through and the sauce thickens and caramelizes.

Transfer the ribs and the sauce to a serving dish and garnish them with the green onions and red chile peppers (if using).

Lemongrass Chicken
Gà Xào Sả Ớt

Serves 4 to 6

This was one of Yen's favorite dishes to eat when she was growing up, and it's a staple in Vietnamese restaurants in America. Because lemongrass is so essential to Vietnamese cuisine, this dish is emblematic of the Vietnamese palate, as well as the simplicity of our homestyle cooking. It can be served over steamed rice.

Ingredients

FOR THE CHICKEN:
Vegetable oil, for frying

30 ounces (850 g) boneless chicken thighs, chopped into bite-size cubes

FOR THE GLAZE:
2 tablespoons vegetable oil

12 cloves garlic, minced

½ cup (40 g) minced lemongrass

6 tablespoons (90 ml) oyster sauce, such as Lee Kum Kee

2 tablespoons chili sauce, such as Huy Fong Chili Garlic Sauce

2 tablespoons fish sauce, such as Three Crabs

2 tablespoons fresh lemon juice (1 medium lemon)

6 tablespoons (75 g) sugar

Ground black pepper

FOR SERVING:
½ red onion, sliced

¼ bunch cilantro, leaves and stems chopped

2 Fresno chiles, sliced

1 lime, cut into wedges

Method

Fry the chicken: In a 3-quart (3-L) saucepan, add enough oil to the pan to fill halfway (about ½ cup / 120 ml). Bring the oil to high heat. When the oil starts to gently bubble, reduce to medium heat. Add the chicken and fry for 8 to 10 minutes, until golden brown and crisp. Set aside.

Glaze the chicken: Discard the oil and clean the pan. In the same pan, bring 2 tablespoons oil to high heat. Add the garlic and lemongrass, then reduce the heat to medium-low. When the garlic and lemongrass crisp up and are fragrant, in about 30 seconds, add the fried chicken and toss to coat in the fragrant oil. Add the oyster sauce, chili sauce, fish sauce, lemon juice, sugar, and black pepper. Bring to high heat and mix all the ingredients together until the sauce thickens and caramelizes.

Serve the lemongrass chicken on a plate with the red onions, cilantro, and sliced chile. Squeeze a lime wedge over the top and serve.

Thịt kho is a slow-braised, caramelized pork dish–like a stew–that is arguably one of the most elemental and essential homestyle dishes in Vietnamese cuisine. It also helped convince Yen to date me! After moving from Houston to New York, Yen, who had grown up eating this dish all the time, didn't know where to find a good version of it, so I invited her to my house. My mom made it for her and it was our first meal all together. For us, this dish is the taste of home. While our recipe calls for a Dutch oven, this dish is often cooked and served in a clay pot. You may choose to serve it in a clay pot, which will keep it warm and lend a traditional touch to your table.

Caramelized Pork Belly with Egg
Thịt Kho Trứng
Serves 6 to 8

Method

Fill a large bowl with ice and water and set aside. Place the eggs in a large pot and add water to cover the eggs by 1 inch (2.5 cm). Over high heat, bring the water to a rapid boil and cook the eggs for 8 minutes. Remove the eggs from the boiling water and submerge them in the prepared ice bath. Once the eggs are cool enough to comfortably handle, peel off the shells and set the eggs aside on a plate.

Heat the vegetable oil in a high-sided pot, such as a Dutch oven, over high heat. When the oil is hot, add the garlic and shallots and cook, stirring often, until golden brown, about 5 minutes. Add the pork belly to the pot and lightly sear on both sides, about 2½ minutes per side. Add the fish sauce, oyster sauce, dark soy sauce, rock sugar, salt, and chicken bouillon, mixing constantly until all the ingredients are combined and the rock sugar has dissolved, 3 to 5 minutes.

Reduce the heat to a simmer, add 3 cups (720 ml) water to the pot and the reserved peeled eggs, and bring the braising liquid to a boil. Reduce to medium heat and cook for about 40 minutes, until the liquid has reduced and thickened and the pork is medium soft. Both the pork and the eggs will take on a brown color from the sauce. (If a thinner sauce is preferred, reduce the braising liquid over a lower heat or for less time.)

Meanwhile, slice the chiles and thinly slice the green onions. When the braising liquid has reached your desired consistency, serve the pork and eggs topped with green onions and chiles and jasmine rice and pickled vegetables, if using, on the side.

Ingredients

12 to 16 large eggs (2 per portion)

½ cup (120 ml) vegetable oil

2½ tablespoons minced garlic

2 tablespoons minced shallots

1¾ pounds (800 g) pork belly, sliced ¾-inch (2-cm) thick by 1½-inches (4-cm) long

¼ cup (60 ml) fish sauce, such as Three Crabs

¼ cup (60 ml) oyster sauce, such as Lee Kum Kee

¼ cup (60 ml) dark soy sauce, such as Pearl River Bridge

½ cup (70 g) rock sugar

1 teaspoon kosher salt

2 tablespoons chicken bouillon, such as Totole Granulated Chicken Soup Base Mix

2 Fresno chiles

1 bunch green onions

4 cups (520 g) cooked white jasmine rice

Pickled Vegetables (page 45) and/or store-bought pickled mustard greens and leeks, such as Pigeon (optional)

Cá kho is one of the culinary hallmarks of the Mekong Delta region in southern Vietnam, an area known for its abundance of seafood. Traditionally braised in the Vietnamese clay pot, it produces an intense, flavorful sauce as the juices of the fish caramelize with the sugar and other ingredients such as oyster sauce and soy sauce. We make our version in a regular frying pan, which still brings out the same flavors as a clay pot but can be cooked more precisely. However, we do like to serve the dish in a preheated clay pot, since it holds heat so well. We get our fish cut at the seafood counter of our supermarket. We like serving this with Sour Soup with Shrimp, or Canh Chua Tôm (page 107), which is from the same region in southern Vietnam.

. SEAFOOD .

Caramelized Fish
Cá Kho Tộ

Serves 4 to 6

Method

Heat 12-inch (30-cm) nonstick frying pan to high and add ⅓ cup (75 ml) vegetable oil to cover the bottom of the pan. Place all the fish pieces into the pan. Sear each piece for 2 minutes on two sides, then set the cooked pieces aside on paper towels to drain any excess oil.

Preheat the same pan to high heat, leaving in the remaining oil. Add the fish sauce, oyster sauce, dark soy sauce, ½ cup (120 ml) water, the sugar, and pepper. Bring to a boil, then add the drained fish and cook for about 5 minutes, until the sauce reduces and caramelizes.

If using a clay pot for serving, bring the clay pot to high heat for 3 minutes and then remove it from the heat. Use a spatula to transfer the fish to the heated clay pot or a deep-dish plate or bowl for serving. Pour the sauce over the top.

Garnish with the crispy fried garlic, red chile, and green onion. Serve with steamed rice on the side.

Ingredients

Vegetable oil, for frying

1½ pounds (680 g) Chilean seabass, cut into 2-inch (5-cm) cubes

3 tablespoons fish sauce, such as Three Crabs

2 tablespoons oyster sauce, such as Lee Kum Kee

½ tablespoon dark soy sauce, such as Pearl River Bridge

¼ cup (50 g) sugar

1 tablespoon freshly ground black pepper

¼ cup (26 g) Crispy Fried Garlic (page 63)

1 red Thai chile, sliced

1 green onion, sliced

Steamed white jasmine rice, for serving

The bedrock of Vietnamese social life is nhậu culture–the ritual of gathering over snackable food and plentiful drink. These everyday celebrations take place all over the streets of Vietnam. To nhậu is to eat with your hands and wash it all down with ice-cold beers. It's the sound of glasses clinking along with screams of "một, hai, ba, dzo!" ("one, two, three, cheers!").

Shellfish are among the most popular nhậu dishes, from snails to mussels and clams. My dad's personal favorite is razor clams, which offer a balanced texture that's more buttery than chewy. When grilled, they have an amazing, charred taste that is perfect with a sauce like our Tamarind Sauce (page 48), our Salt, Pepper, and Lime Dip (page 64), and red Thai chiles.

If you're unable to get access to razor clams, you can make this dish with littleneck clams, Manila clams, or scallops on the shell (grill them the same way until they pop open).

This recipe originated from an attempt to impress my dad that employed a topping of green onion oil, chopped peanuts, and crispy shallots. The herb that completes the dish is Vietnamese coriander, which is worth hunting down at an Asian supermarket. The clams should be enjoyed right away, but the sauce can be stored in an airtight container in the refrigerator for up to a week.

Grilled Razor Clams
Ốc Móng Tay Nướng

Serves 4 to 6

recipe continued

Ingredients

FOR THE RAZOR CLAMS:

2 pounds (910 g) razor clams

1½ teaspoons kosher salt, plus more for cleaning the clams

⅓ cup (80 g)minced garlic

8 ounces (225 g) fresh Vietnamese coriander or basil, stems removed

½ cup (120 ml) vegetable oil

1 tablespoon sugar

1 teaspoon monosodium glutamate (MSG)

FOR SERVING:

1 bunch Vietnamese coriander and/or basil

½ cup (70 g) chopped roasted peanuts

½ cup (120 ml) Green Onion Oil (page 55)

Crispy Fried Shallots (page 61)

Tamarind Sauce (page 48)

Method

Make the razor clams: Put the clams in a bowl and run cold water over the bowl until the clams are completely submerged. Add a big pinch of salt and set the razor clams aside to soak for 15 minutes, allowing them to release any sand from their shells. Rinse each clam three or four more times under cold running water to cleanse them fully.

In a food processor, add the garlic, Vietnamese coriander, vegetable oil, sugar, 1½ teaspoons salt, and MSG. Process for 3 to 4 minutes on a high setting until the ingredients are thoroughly incorporated and the sauce is thick.

Heat a gas grill to high heat. Place the clams on the grate and cook for about 2 minutes, until the shells open. Spoon the sauce into the open clams and grill for another 2 to 3 minutes, allowing the sauce to cook into the clams, heat, and become fragrant. Discard any clams that have not opened.

Serve: Top the grilled clams with the loose leaves of Vietnamese coriander, peanuts, a drizzle of green onion oil, and crispy shallots. Scoop the meat of the clam out of the shell with all the toppings for the perfect bite. Serve with an additional bunch of Vietnamese coriander in case diners want more (we always do) and the tamarind sauce for dipping.

Tangy and bright, tamarind plays a significant role in Southeast Asian cooking. One of our favorite dishes to make with these fruit pods is cua rang me (literally "crab sautéed in tamarind"). A balance of sweet, sour, and savory flavors, this dish is a must-make for seafood lovers—we particularly enjoy the way the tamarind amplifies the richness of crab fat, which is used in the sauce for the dish. In typical Vietnamese fashion, we're using all parts of the crab, including the crab's soft organs, known as crab fat or tomalley. This green substance, which turns yellow-orange when cooked, is found in both the top shell and body of the crab, and packs a ton of umami shellfish flavor.

This recipe comes from Yen's mom, who is from the city of Rach Giá in southern Vietnam. When I visited Yen's family in Mississippi for the first time, this is what her mom made for me. It blew my mind, and I still remember canceling our dinner reservations to stay home and eat it. This dish is one that can be enjoyed by itself, with a cold beer, but it can also be heaped over spoonfuls of steamed rice. We don't crack the crabs for our guests—we prefer they get their hands dirty and enjoy the full finger-licking flavor of the sauce. If you prefer to use smaller crabs, that is okay, just make sure to use the same weight (around 4 pounds / 1.8 kg total) so that the flavor and number of servings are the same, and when preparing the crabs, cut them into only four pieces, instead of six.

Tamarind Crab
Cua Rang Me

Serves 4 to 6

recipe continued

Ingredients

4 pounds (1.8 kg) Dungeness crabs (about 3 crabs)

1 cup (100 g) tempura flour, such as Kim Tu Thap Tempura Batter Mix

⅓ cup (80 ml) vegetable oil

½ cup (120 g) minced garlic

1 teaspoon kosher salt

5 tablespoons sugar

1 teaspoon monosodium glutamate MSG

2 shallots, thinly sliced

1 teaspoon ground black pepper

2 tablespoons fish sauce, such as Three Crabs

1 teaspoon chicken bouillon, such as Totole Granulated Chicken Soup Base Mix

1 tablespoon onion powder

1 tablespoon red chile powder

2 tablespoons crab paste, such as Por Kwan

2 tablespoons tamarind concentrate, such as Cock Brand Concentrate Cooking Tamarind

1 bunch green onions, thinly sliced, for garnish

Method

Line the bottom of a large bowl with a double layer of paper towels to soak up excess water and fluid from the crabs.

First remove the top shell from a crab and set aside for presentation purposes. Then, extract the tomalley from the top of the shell and the body, using your hands or a small spoon to remove all the soft green substance. Farther back in the tail, you may also find eggs, which are black in color. Remove these as well. Set the eggs and tomalley aside.

Chop the body down the middle lengthwise, and then break that down with three more chops until you have six pieces. Place all the chopped pieces in the lined bowl. Prepare the remaining crabs in the same way. Batter the crab in the tempura flour in a large mixing bowl.

In a medium saucepan, add enough oil to fill the pan halfway and bring to high heat. When the oil starts to gently bubble and reaches 350°F (175°C), when measured with an instant-read thermometer, add the battered crab and fry for 4 to 5 minutes, until golden brown and airy crisp. Remove the fried crab and repeat until it's all fried, including the crab shell top, and place on paper towels to drain the excess oil.

Add the oil to a large wok and bring to medium-high heat. Add the minced garlic to the heated pan and cook until golden, about 3 minutes, stirring often to avoid burning.

Add the pieces of crab and their empty top shells and mix thoroughly with the garlic. Cook for 3 to 4 minutes, until the crab shells turn red. Add the salt, sugar, MSG, shallots, ground black pepper, fish sauce, chicken bouillon, onion powder, chili powder, crab paste, tamarind concentrate, and tomalley. Stir and bring to a boil for about 8 minutes, until the sauce is reduced by half and the dish is fragrant.

Serve the crab in a large serving dish, topped with the chopped green onions. Add the top shells for presentation, as shown in the photo, if you desire.

Madame Vo Lobster Special

Serves 4 to 6

Presented with all the pieces of a whole fried lobster sitting on a bed of noodles, our lobster special at Madame Vo is an off-menu item that customers must pre-order twenty-four hours in advance. Salty, sweet, and decadent with butter, it's inspired partly by the famous lobster dish at Newport Seafood Restaurant in San Gabriel, California. This was one of my favorite restaurants and dishes when I was growing up, and my family always ordered it when we visited California.

For Madame Vo, I put my own spin on the dish, using just my flavor memories and adding a good amount of fish sauce and sesame oil. We use female lobsters specifically because they contain eggs and tomalley, or the lobster's soft organs, which are also sometimes referred to as lobster fat. This ingredient contributes a brininess and richness to the sauce.

The lobster is chopped and fried shell-on. So, when ready to enjoy, use your hands, forks, or chopsticks to pick the lobster meat out of the shell, then twirl it up in the thick lo mein noodles for the full experience.

Method

Prep the lobster: Gather a cleaver, scissors, and a chopstick. Use the chopstick to pierce one hole in the center of the squishy, white bottom of the lobster, near the tail, to release the water and drain. Then, use the cleaver to cleanly chop off the lobster head, separating it from the body. Using the scissors, trim the antennae off the head and discard. From the lobster head, extract the tomalley, which can be identified by a yellow-green color and runny texture, into a bowl using your finger or a teaspoon. Set the head aside to be used in the final presentation, if desired. You can opt to use scissors to remove the legs from the body and tail and discard them, since they don't contain a lot of meat, or leave them on, as you prefer. Use scissors to remove the feathery gills, which stick out from the upper-middle section of the cavity, and discard them.

Chop the lobster: Using a butcher knife, halve the lobster body crosswise, then cut each half crosswise in half again to yield four pieces. Use a spoon to remove any visible eggs, which are a dark gray to black color, and scoop them into the bowl with the tomalley. With the same knife, cut the claws away from the body and halve each claw lengthwise. Dry the cut pieces of lobster with a clean kitchen towel, then place the lobster pieces, including the head, in a large mixing bowl, add the tempura flour, and mix to evenly coat.

Deep-fry the lobster: Fill a 6-quart (6-L) pot halfway with vegetable oil and bring to high heat (375°F/190°C), when measured with an instant-read thermometer—you will see the oil start to bubble. Line a baking sheet with parchment paper or a paper towel to soak up any excess oil. Working in batches as needed to avoid overcrowding, add the lobster pieces, including the head, to the hot oil. Fry four to five pieces at a time, depending on the size of your pot and lobster, and turn the head over halfway through to cook it on all sides. Turn the heat down to medium (325°F/165°C). Deep-fry for 5 to 10 minutes more, depending on how crispy you'd like the lobster to be. Use tongs to remove the lobster from the oil, place on the prepared baking sheet, and set aside to drain.

Make the sauce: Bring a 12-inch (30-cm) wok or large frying pan to high heat and then add ¼ cup (60 ml) vegetable oil. Cook the garlic and jalapeños in the oil for 3 to 4 minutes, or until the garlic turns golden brown. Reduce the temperature to medium low and add the oyster sauce, fish sauce, sesame oil, sugar, and ground black pepper, stir to combine, then cook for 1 minute. Add the lobster pieces, bring to a high heat, and toss to bind the sauce to the lobster, 3 to 4 minutes. Remove from the heat and set aside.

Meanwhile, make the noodles: Fill a 3-quart (3-L) pot with about 2 quarts (2 L) water and bring to a boil. Add the noodles and boil for 3 to 4 minutes, until soft, then drain the noodles and rinse under cold water.

Assemble and serve: Using the same wok or frying pan used to make the sauce, add ¼ cup (60 ml) vegetable oil, bring to high heat, and add the reserved lobster eggs and tomalley. Cook for 2 to 3 minutes until the eggs turn red. Add the noodles and green onions and toss to combine. Plate the noodles on a large serving dish and arrange the lobster and sauce on top of the noodles, adding the lobster head as a decoration.

Ingredients

FOR THE LOBSTER:

1 (3-pound/1.4-kg) or 2 (1½-pound/680-g) female lobsters

2 cups (210 g) tempura flour, such as Kim Tu Thap Tempura Batter Mix

Vegetable oil, for frying

FOR THE SAUCE:

Vegetable oil

3 tablespoons minced garlic

2 jalapeño chiles, chopped

3 tablespoons oyster sauce, such as Lee Kum Kee

¼ cup (60 ml) fish sauce, such as Three Crabs

2 tablespoons sesame oil

½ cup (100 g) sugar

2 tablespoons ground black pepper

FOR THE NOODLES:

1 (16-ounce/455-g) bag dried lo mein egg noodles, such as Twin Marquis

FOR SERVING:

4 cups (220 g) chopped green onions (about 9 bunches)

CLOCKWISE FROM TOP: Hanoi-Style Tumeric Fish (page 190), Tamarind Crab (page 183), Grilled Razor Clams (page 181), Madame Vo Lobster Special (page 186)

Hanoi-Style Turmeric Fish
Chả Cá La Vong

Serves 3 to 4

Chả cá is a Hanoian specialty dating back more than a century that's typically made with local catfish seasoned with turmeric and garnished with tons of dill. The dish is so beloved that there is an entire street in Hanoi with vendors serving it. When Yen was growing up on the Gulf Coast of Mississippi, where many Vietnamese immigrants are fishermen, including Yen's father, she often had this dish. When we first opened Madame Vo, we didn't have fish on our menu, so when our customers asked for seafood, we decided to adapt this classic recipe and use halibut instead. We offer it as a seasonal special, and people have loved it.

Ingredients

1 (1½-pound/680-g) halibut fillet, cut into quarters

1 teaspoon curry powder

1 teaspoon five-spice powder

1 teaspoon turmeric powder

1 tablespoon kosher salt

1 teaspoon monosodium glutamate (MSG)

1 tablespoon sugar

½ cup (120 g) minced garlic

½ cup (120 ml) vegetable oil, for frying

Freshly ground black pepper

4 to 5 sprigs chopped fresh dill, to taste

¼ cup (14 g) Crispy Fried Shallots (page 61) or store-bought fried shallots, such as Wangderm

1 red Thai chile, sliced

½ cup (120 ml) Vietnamese Dipping Sauce (page 46), for serving

Method

In a medium bowl, add the halibut, curry powder, five-spice powder, turmeric, salt, MSG, sugar, and garlic. Use your hands to evenly spread the spice mixture to coat the halibut pieces on all sides. Wrap the fish in plastic and let sit in the refrigerator for 1 hour or up to overnight.

In a 12-inch (30-cm) frying pan or wok, heat the vegetable oil on high heat. Reduce the heat to medium and pan-sear the fish, cooking for 3 to 5 minutes on each side, until a nice crust develops.

Put the fish on a serving plate, and finish with pepper, chopped dill, fried shallots, and chiles. Serve with a side of nước chấm for dipping.

Stir-Fried Shrimp and Pork Belly
Tôm Rim Thịt Heo

Serves 4 to 6

The combination of shell-on shrimp and pork is quintessentially Vietnamese. This country-style stir-fry is a quick 30-minute meal that was a staple in the weekly dinner rotation for both my parents and Yen's when they were short on time. The magic of the dish comes from the sweet-savory combination of fish sauce and sugar, layered with the richness of the rendered pork fat.

Ingredients

1 pound (455 g) extra-large (16–20 count), head-on shrimp, unpeeled

Vegetable oil, for frying

8 ounces (225 g) pork belly, sliced ¼-inch (6-mm) thick

⅓ cup (80 g) minced garlic

½ tablespoon kosher salt

Ground black pepper

1 teaspoon monosodium glutamate (MSG)

2 tablespoon fish sauce, such as Three Crabs

4 tablespoons sugar

Steamed white jasmine rice, for serving

Method

Leaving the shell on, devein just the top side of each shrimp by piercing a toothpick ⅛ inch (3 mm) deep into the back of the shrimp at the joint between the second and third segments from the head, near the rounded back of the shrimp. Holding the shrimp in your free hand, use the toothpick to lift the black vein. Once it starts to come loose, you can grab it with your hands and pull it out.

In a large skillet, heat ⅓ cup (80 ml) vegetable oil on high heat. Sear the pork belly in the oil for about 2½ minutes per side, or until crispy. Reduce the heat to medium low. Add the garlic and continue to fry for 2 to 3 minutes, until the garlic turns golden brown. Add the shrimp, salt, 1 teaspoon pepper, MSG, fish sauce, and sugar. Lower the heat to medium and stir until the pork and shrimp are evenly coated. Cook for about 5 minutes, until a vibrant red sauce comes out of the shrimp heads.

Serve with a pinch ground black pepper and a side of steamed rice.

A sleeper hit on the Madame Vo menu is our lemongrass egg-plant, which is made using a similar process to our stir-fried Lemongrass Chicken (page 172) but yields a spongier and softer, yet still meaty, texture. Vietnamese people traditionally eat vege-tarian on the first day of the Lunar New Year, or Tết, so we initially created this dish partly for that reason. But it's also a great alter-native to the chicken version–ideal for situations where you want something lighter or meatless or both.

Lemongrass Eggplant
Cà Tím Xào Sả Ớt

Serves 4 to 6

Method

Bring a large wok or frying pan to medium low heat and add about 5 tablespoons (75 ml) vegetable oil, enough to cover the bottom of the pan. Cook the garlic and lemongrass in the oil, stirring frequently to avoid burning, for 2 minutes, or until fragrant.

Add the fish sauce, sugar, chili sauce, oyster sauce, and pepper to the pan and stir to combine. Let cook, bubbling, for 1 minute, to allow the sauces to incorporate. Add the eggplant and stir and cook for 3 to 4 minutes. Add the green onions and stir constantly for 2 minutes. Garnish with the red Thai chiles. Serve the eggplant with the steamed rice on the side.

Ingredients

Vegetable oil, for frying

⅓ cup (80 g) minced garlic

3 tablespoons minced lemongrass

¼ cup (60 ml) fish sauce, such as Three Crabs

3 tablespoons sugar

2 tablespoons chili sauce, such as Huy Fong Chili Garlic Sauce

1 teaspoon oyster sauce, such as Lee Kum Kee

Pinch ground black pepper

1 pound (455 g) eggplant, cut on the diagonal into 2-inch-thick (5-cm) slices

1 bunch green onions, chopped into 2-inch (5-cm) pieces

1 to 2 red Thai chiles, sliced, for serving

Steamed jasmine white rice, for serving

Corn is both of our moms' favorite vegetable, so when the family gets together, it's corn all day—in both sweet and salty dishes (see page 206 for Sweet Corn Pudding, one of our favorite corn desserts). This rustic recipe offsets the natural sweetness of the corn with a rich and savory oil made with green onion, a more complex version of the oil you'll see called for throughout this book. Between Yen and I, we could eat a dozen of these ears of corn in one sitting. We recommend enjoying them right away, so that the oil doesn't wilt the corn.

Green Onion Oil Corn on the Cob
Bắp Nướng Mỡ Hành

Serves 6 to 8

Method

Preheat a gas grill to high heat. Grill the corn for about 20 minutes total, rotating the ears every 5 minutes or so to avoid burning and to achieve a nice even char around the entire cob.

Preheat the vegetable oil in a 2-quart (2-L) saucepan over high heat. Once the oil is hot, lower to medium heat and add the butter, sugar, MSG, and salt, stirring to combine. Mix in the green onions and immediately turn off the heat.

Top each ear of grilled corn with 3 to 4 tablespoons green onion oil and serve hot.

Ingredients

8 ears corn, husks and silk removed

½ cup (120 ml) vegetable oil

¼ cup (½ stick; 55 g) unsalted butter

⅓ cup (65 g) sugar

1 teaspoon monosodium glutamate (MSG)

1 teaspoon kosher salt

2½ cups (140 g) chopped green onions (about 4 bunches)

OUR PAST, PRESENT, AND FUTURE

Pushing the Envelope

In Madame Vo's first year, we were blessed to earn the devoted following that continues to support us to this day. Soon after Sarah Jessica Parker's fateful visit to the restaurant, we got our first *New York Times* coverage. We had opened at the same time as another Vietnamese restaurant that focused on northern Vietnamese food in contrast to our southern, Saigonese style, so the article focused on that.

Naturally, it was the incredible Ligaya Mishan who put it best: "Each phở is beautiful. There is room enough for both." And just like that, more American consumers became aware of the vast regional differences in Vietnamese food.

More headlines followed: in *Eater*, *Bloomberg*, *Grubstreet*, *Vice*, and one of my personal favorites that's framed in the restaurant: *Hypebeast*. It was around this moment that we knew there was no turning back: We were representing Vietnamese culture at a national—and even global—level. From doing video series for *Vice*, *Saveur*, and *Business Insider*, to getting featured in *Vogue Korea*, we're immensely grateful for the platform we've been given to share our tried-and-true home cooking with the world.

After the media coverage, our following has grown exponentially, our staff T-shirts routinely sell out online, and our special events are always completely booked. It's helped that we've also earned a bit of a celebrity following, with visits from the likes of Calvin Klein, Alan Cumming, Daniel Craig, and others—not to mention countless stars in the global Vietnamese community, ranging from Miss Universe Vietnam and Saigon-based interior designer Thai Cong to Vietnamese American pop star Thuy and influencer Twaydabae.

It might be said that the year we opened is when the Vietnamese food revolution in NYC began. After all, since 2017, plenty of modern Vietnamese restaurants, bakeries, and coffee shops and brands have opened, each focusing on a different aspect of the cuisine, introducing NYC diners to a myriad of new dishes and drinks. One common thread among these: Their menus feature prices that are a far cry from the prices in Chinatown.

We didn't set out to change the game. We just did it because it was what was authentic and right to us. Why shouldn't phở—with its labor-intensive preparation and hours of simmering—not be priced as much as a plate of pasta, or a bowl of ramen? And while we weren't alone in the effort to change New Yorkers' perceptions of Vietnamese food, we're proud of the stand we took to price our food fairly, and to not compromise on quality.

In 2018, we got pregnant again, and in 2019 we welcomed our second son, Clinton, just after opening our second restaurant, Madame Vo BBQ, a Vietnamese barbecue restaurant, on the corner of East Sixth Street and Second Avenue. Featuring meat cooked on tabletop grills, it became the first Vietnamese restaurant to be reviewed by *New York Times* restaurant critic Pete Wells. For a while, we had a good run, introducing New Yorkers to the art of Vietnamese grilling (page 160).

Then came 2020, and the pandemic. We all know that story, so we won't belabor the point. We were able to keep the Madame Vo flagship open with takeout and delivery, making just enough to retain some of our staff and donate thousands of meals to help healthcare heroes. But at Madame Vo BBQ, the interactive, in-person dining experience was impossible to translate to a remote format. So, in 2021, we decided to close the Vietnamese barbecue outpost. It was a difficult time for everyone in New York City, and we bonded with our fellow small business owners who faced similar tough decisions.

As COVID-era restrictions lifted and life began to return to normal, we were hungry to do something big. Since we still had the space that formerly housed Madame Vo BBQ, we started to redevelop the menu and plan a redesign of the space, taking out the tabletop grills to create a more open format with more seating.

On September 13, 2022, we opened Monsieur Vo—a modern Vietnamese restaurant that paid homage to the uncles, brothers, fathers, and other Vietnamese men in our lives. Unlike our flagship, which focuses on noodle soups and homestyle dishes largely passed down from our moms,

Monsieur Vo goes beyond tradition, taking inspiration from Vietnamese ăn nhậu gastropub culture, which reminds us of the men in our lives. Here, we also showcase large-format meats like a whole beef shank in bone marrow gravy and a sauce inspired by the Central Vietnamese lemongrass soup, Bún Bò Huế (page 135).

As we write this book in 2023, we can already see that New Yorkers and tourists alike are more ready than ever before to try Vietnamese foods that lie outside the spectrum of phở and bánh mì. People used to think you could only find Vietnamese food in Chinatown: Now, you can go to the Upper West Side for bánh chung and go to Williamsburg for Hanoian turmeric fish. Or you can come to Monsieur Vo for beef tartare inspired by bò tái chanh, a citrus-cured beef carpaccio.

Being a native New Yorker, I've been blessed to see how the city has evolved and be a part of that change in my own way. Raising our kids and building our business here, Yen and I are grateful that we could see the day when Vietnamese food has become a beloved staple of New York City cuisine in its own right. And the city is better off for it.

As for the Madame Vo journey, we've only just scratched the surface. We're driven and energized by the desire to continue pushing the envelope of Vietnamese cuisine, sharing what we love with all those who walk into our doors. We're blessed that you're allowing us to share our passion with you, and we hope that soon, you'll be making your own memories, and telling your own stories, through Vietnamese food.

On Vietnamese Desserts and Drinks
"Một, hai, ba, yo!"

Desserts

Vietnamese desserts are known for their often-bright colors, contrasting textures, and refreshing qualities. In line with broader Vietnamese culinary philosophy (see page 24), they are characterized by a balance and harmony of flavors and textures and are notably moderate in their sweetness. Indeed, when tasting a Vietnamese dessert, saying, "Not too sweet," is a great compliment.

Because of the hot weather in Vietnam, many of our desserts have the option to be served cold. This includes many variations of chè, a loosely defined category of treats best described as "dessert soups" due to the consistency of ingredients: solid chunks of fruit, jellies, and beans floating in coconut milk. Many Vietnamese desserts are meant to be refreshing, like the shaved iced dessert called Chè Thái (page 205) and the grass jelly dessert Sương Sa Hạt Lựu (page 213), which is often said to reduce heat within the body.

Coffee and Smoothies

Café culture is big in Vietnam, which is the world's second-largest producer of coffee. Historically, at cafés in Vietnam, people often spend hours to enjoy coffee over conversation, rather than grabbing it in a rush to-go. At many coffee shops, you'll find Vietnamese coffee, both traditional like ours (page 225) as well as modern versions.

Thanks to Vietnam's bounty of tropical fruits, cafés also typically serve smoothies made with tropical fruit like avocado (page 228), coconut (page 231), and durian (page 231). It's worth noting that avocado is often seen as a sweet rather than savory ingredient, especially when combined with condensed milk.

Cocktails

Vietnam has a storied drinking culture that started with various fermented rice wines and distilled liquors made from glutinous rice. In the modern era, for casual drinking, Vietnam is more of a beer country. That said, in recent years, cocktail bars in Vietnam, as well as at modern Vietnamese American restaurants like ours, have been shaking things up, putting a Vietnamese spin on classic cocktails like the espresso martini (page 226) and creating originals like the Madame Sour (page 234) on our menu.

How to Say "Cheers" in Vietnamese!

The way to say "Cheers" in Vietnamese is "Một, hai, ba, dzo!" which literally means: "One, two, three, in!" Whether you're at a local nhậu restaurant or at a Vietnamese wedding, you'll periodically hear a whole table stand up and yell, "Một hai ba, yo!"

On the Vietnamese American Moment

Our friend Thuy, the talented singer-songwriter

In the years since we first opened Madame Vo, Vietnamese food is not the only industry that has reached new heights. Though we're grateful to every person who visits Madame Vo and Monsieur Vo, we feel a particularly deep sense of pride to have served Vietnamese people—and Asian people in general—who are leading their fields, both in Vietnam and in America.

As more young Vietnamese Americans come of age, we're seeing inspirational figures like Amanda Nguyen, who was nominated for a Nobel Peace Prize in 2019 for helping to pass federal legislation advocating for survivors of sexual violence, as well as award-winning Vietnamese American authors, like Pulitzer Prize winner Viet Thanh Nguyen, whose debut novel, *The Sympathizer*, has become an HBO scripted series.

In entertainment, we acknowledge those Vietnamese and Vietnam-born actors and actresses who are breaking the bamboo ceiling in film, from the inimitable Ke Huy Quan of *Everything Everywhere All at Once*, *The Menu's* Hong Chau to *Star Wars'* Kelly Marie Tran, who made history when she wore the traditional Vietnamese dress, ao dai, on the red carpet at the 2022 Oscars. Then there's the music industry, where we're seeing Vietnamese American singers like Keshi, Dolly Ave, and our friend Thuy making waves on the charts.

In the world of fashion, we've been excited to see the rise of Vietnamese designers like Peter Do, Bach Mai of Bach Mai, and Thai Nguyen come to the forefront. Generally speaking, it's never been more exciting to be a Vietnamese person in America.

Yen's mom used to have a shake and dessert stand when she lived in Rạch Giá, a port city in southwest Vietnam. Loaded to the brim with tropical fruits, toddy palm seeds, jellies, and coconut milk, this Thai-influenced shaved ice dessert was a bestseller–it's a perfect dessert to enjoy on a sweltering summer day. While it can be hard to find fresh lychee and longan in the States, using the canned versions works pretty well. The dessert also contains water chestnuts, which offer a bit of nutty flavor and the texture of an apple. We dye them red just because the added color is fun.

Thai Mixed Fruit Shaved Ice Dessert
Chè Thái

Serves 4 to 6

Method

Prepare the water chestnuts: Pour 4 cups (960 ml) ice water into a large bowl and set it aside. In a heatproof bowl, add the diced water chestnuts and a few drops of red food coloring until the red hue is evenly distributed. Slowly add the tapioca flour to the diced water chestnuts and make sure each cube is fully coated. Boil enough water to cover the water chestnut mixture in the bowl, and gently pour it over the top. Once the water chestnuts float to the top of the bowl, scoop them out with a slotted spoon and add them to the prepared bowl of ice water. Keep the water chestnuts in the ice water for 8 to 10 minutes, then remove them with a slotted spoon. Make sure all excess water is drained and set aside the water chestnuts on paper towels.

Make the simple syrup and candy the chestnuts: In a medium bowl, add the sugar to 1 cup (240 ml) boiling water and stir until the sugar has completely dissolved. Once the quartered water chestnuts have dried completely, add them to the simple syrup mixture and gently stir to coat. Set aside while you prepare the filling.

Make the filling: If you're using fresh ingredients, cut the jackfruit, palm seeds, and coconut meat into 3- to 4-inch-long (7.5- to 10-cm) strips. If you're using canned jackfruit and canned palm seeds, cut both ingredients into strips. If you're using canned coconut jelly, cut the jelly into dice-size cubes, if it isn't already cubed. Cut the pandan jelly into 1-inch (2.5-cm) cubes. If you're using canned ai-yu jelly, simply open the can and cut the jelly into 1-inch (2.5-cm) cubes.

Assemble: Add about ⅓ cup (50 to 80 g) each of the jackfruit, palm seed, coconut meat or coconut jelly, pandan jelly, lychee, and longan into each tall serving glass. (Feel free to add more or less of each ingredient, depending on your taste preferences.) Using a slotted spoon, add the reserved candied water chestnuts. Pour in the half-and-half, top with crushed ice, and enjoy immediately.

Ingredients

FOR THE WATER CHESTNUTS:
15 to 18 fresh or canned water chestnuts, quartered

Red liquid food coloring

1 cup (135 g) tapioca flour or starch

FOR THE SIMPLE SYRUP:
1 cup (200 g) sugar

FOR THE FILLINGS:
20 ounces (560 g) fresh or canned jackfruit, drained

20 ounces (560 g) fresh or canned toddy palm seeds, drained

20 ounces (560 g) fresh or canned coconut meat or jelly, drained

1 (19-ounce/540-g) can pandan jelly, such as Mong Lee Shang, drained

1 (19-ounce/540-g) can ai-yu jelly, such as Chin Chin, drained

TO ASSEMBLE:
20 ounces (560 g) fresh or canned lychee, drained

20 ounces (560 g) fresh or canned longan, drained

1 cup (240 ml) half-and-half

Crushed ice

Sweet Corn Pudding
Chè Bắp

Serves 4 to 6

Beyond savory dishes, corn can also be found in many Vietnamese dessert offerings like chè–a category of desserts best described as pudding or, in some cases, sweet soup. Though you can make chè with tons of different ingredients, from taro to mung beans, the go-to in my family is the corn version. My mom took great pride in choosing the best ears of corn at the market based on the warmth of their color, their size, or their juiciness. Made with coconut milk, this is a dessert that works well for special diets since it is naturally vegan, gluten-free, and dairy-free.

For added complexity of taste, you may add pandan, which is frequently used as a dessert flavoring because of its natural sweetness and notes of almond and rose. Pandan leaves, found fresh or frozen at an Asian supermarket, are preferred over extract if you can find them, as their flavor is lighter and more delicate, but extract is a good alternative. This pudding can be served hot or cold.

Method

Make the sweet rice: In a bowl, cover the rice in water and let soak for 1 hour. Drain the rice, place in a large pot, and pour in 4½ cups (1 L) water. Cook the rice on medium low for about 30 minutes, until the rice has a sticky and soft texture and is fully cooked.

Make the pudding base: One at a time, stand each ear of corn up in a large bowl and, holding the ear steady, run a sharp cleaver or chef's knife down the length of the cob to cut off the kernels, rotating the cob as you go until all the kernels are in the bowl. Set the kernels aside and reserve the cobs for the next step.

To make a pandan-infused corn water, combine the corn cobs, pandan leaves (if using; wash beforehand), and 2 cups (480 ml) water in a 3-quart (3-L) pot and bring to a boil. Cover the pot, reduce the heat to a low simmer, and let simmer for 30 minutes. Turn off the heat. Using tongs, remove the corn cobs and pandan leaves (if using) and discard. Set the mixture aside.

Meanwhile, place the tapioca pearls in a small bowl, cover with cold water by ½ inch (12 mm), and let the pearls soak for 15 minutes, then drain and set aside.

In a 2-quart (2-L) saucepan, bring the coconut milk to a boil and let thicken for 1 minute. Add the thickened coconut milk, reserved corn kernels, sugar, and a pinch of salt to the pot with the corn cob and pandan leaves mixture, stirring to combine. Return the mixture to a boil and then lower the heat to a simmer and cook for about 10 minutes, until the corn kernels are tender. Taste and adjust the flavor with more sugar and salt, as needed.

Stir in the soaked tapioca pearls and let simmer until soft, 2 to 5 minutes, or according to package instructions. Add the reserved sweet rice and bring the mixture up to a boil for an additional 2 minutes. Remove the pot from the heat and allow the pudding to cool slightly.

Serve warm in bowls or glasses or refrigerate and serve cold (either way works!). If desired, garnish with sesame seeds and coconut milk just before serving.

Ingredients

FOR THE SWEET RICE:
1 cup (220 g) sweet rice, such as Mei Gui Hua

FOR THE PUDDING BASE:
5 to 6 ears of corn, husks and silks removed

4 fresh or frozen pandan leaves or 2 teaspoons pandan extract (optional)

1 cup (150 g) small tapioca pearls

1 (14-ounce/400-ml) can coconut milk, such as Aroy-D

¾ cup (150 g) sugar, plus more to taste

Kosher salt

FOR SERVING:
¼ cup (40 g) toasted sesame seeds (optional)

Coconut milk (optional)

Taro Sweet Soup
Chè Khoai Môn

Serves 4 to 6

Chè khoai môn is a hearty and traditional Vietnamese taro pudding that combines the root vegetable with sticky rice topped with coconut milk. (Think potato soup, but sweet.) Cubes of taro are steamed until soft, then sweetened with sugar. Served hot or cold, it's a versatile dessert to make and enjoy year-round. You can store this taro pudding for 2 to 3 days in an airtight container in the refrigerator (but don't add the coconut milk until serving time).

Ingredients

1¼ cups (250 g) sweet rice

2 cups (400 g) taro, cut into ½-inch (12-mm) cubes

1 (14-ounce/400-ml) can coconut milk, such as Aroy-D

1½ teaspoons kosher salt

2 cups (400 g) sugar

¼ cup (40 g) toasted sesame seeds (optional)

Method

In a large bowl, cover the sweet rice in water and let soak for 1 hour to soften. Drain the rice, place in a large pot, and pour in 4½ cups (1 L) water. Cook the rice, uncovered, on medium-low for about 30 minutes, until the rice has a sticky, soft texture and is fully cooked.

Add enough water to a 2-quart (2-L) saucepan to fill the pan halfway and bring to a boil on high heat. Add the taro and cook for about 5 minutes, until the taro softens. The cubes of taro should still hold their shape but be easy to smash with pressure (you can test this by placing one piece on a cutting board or plate and pushing down on it with a fork). Using a spider or fine-mesh strainer, scoop the taro from the water, set aside on a plate to cool, and discard the cooking liquid.

In the same pan, bring the coconut milk to a boil. Mix in the salt, turn off the heat, and set aside.

In a 6-quart (6-L) saucepan, add 4 cups (960 ml) water, the sweet rice, taro, and sugar. Cook for 15 minutes on high heat or until the mixture comes to a boil, then turn off the heat.

To serve warm, immediately ladle the pudding into individual serving bowls and top with the coconut milk. If enjoying cold, refrigerate the coconut milk until serving time, then pour over the top. Sprinkle with sesame seeds before serving.

Tricolor Dessert
Chè Ba Màu

Serves 6 to 8

This classic shaved ice dessert always reminds me of Phở Bang, the OG phở restaurant located on Mott Street in Manhattan's Chinatown, which is where we used to go on Sundays when I was a kid. This treat is named for its unique layers of green, yellow, and red, which always made it stand out in the glass case that displayed the sweets. I love to eat it in a tall, clear glass with a long spoon so I can watch as the colors and ingredients—which include red bean and coconut—fuse together. If you feel like you want to save a portion of the ingredients for later, all the various components—agar-agar jelly, mung bean paste, red beans, and coconut milk sauce—may be refrigerated in separate airtight containers for up to a week.

Method

Make the green agar-agar jelly: Wash the pandan leaves. In a food processor on the puree setting, grind the pandan leaves with 2 cups (480 ml) water, and then filter the green mixture through a fine-mesh sieve or cheesecloth to make an extract.

In a 2-quart (2-L) saucepan, mix the agar-agar powder with 3⅓ cups (800 ml) cold water and cook over medium heat for 3 to 4 minutes, stirring continuously until the agar-agar melts. Add the sugar to the agar-agar mixture and cook for 1 minute, or until the sugar dissolves. Add the pandan leaf extract and cook for about 2 minutes, stirring constantly until the mixture turns translucent green.

Pour the agar-agar mixture into a 9 by 5-inch (23 by 12-cm) loaf pan and chill in the refrigerator for about 3 hours (or overnight), or until the mixture is jellied. Cut the jelly into 3- to 4-inch-long (7.5- to 10-cm) strips.

Make the bean pastes: Fill two bowls with water and add the mung beans to one and the red beans to the other. Let soak overnight.

In a 2-quart (2-L) saucepan, combine the mung beans with 2 cups (480 ml) water over high heat and bring to a boil. Stir in ¼ cup (50 g) of the sugar and cook the beans until tender, about 30 minutes. Transfer the cooked mung beans to a bowl or a blender and mash or blend the beans into a smooth paste; let cool in the refrigerator.

Using the same pot, combine the red beans with 3 cups (720 ml) water and bring to a boil over high heat. Stir in the other ½ cup (100 g) sugar and cook for about 45 minutes, until the beans are soft but retain their shape and are not mushy. Transfer the cooked red beans to a bowl or blender and mash or blend them into a smooth paste; let cool in the refrigerator.

Make the coconut milk sauce: In a 2-quart (2-L) saucepan over medium heat, add the coconut milk, cornstarch, sugar, and salt and cook for 2 to 3 minutes, until the mixture boils and thickens. Turn off the heat and let cool at room temperature.

Assemble and serve: In tall 12-ounce (360-ml) glasses, add a spoonful of red bean paste, followed by a spoonful of mung bean paste, followed by a spoonful of agar-agar jelly. Top each dessert with coconut milk sauce and ½ cup (115 g) shaved ice. Each serving should be separated into distinct colors, like a layer cake. Serve with long spoons, which can be used to mix all the ingredients before digging in.

Ingredients

FOR THE GREEN AGAR-AGAR JELLY:
3 fresh or frozen pandan leaves

5 tablespoons agar-agar powder, such as Telephŏne

¼ cup (50 g) sugar

FOR THE BEAN PASTES:
¾ cup (145 g) peeled split mung beans, such as SunVoi

1½ cups (295 g) dried red adzuki beans

¾ cup (150 g) sugar

FOR THE COCONUT MILK SAUCE:
1 cup (8 ounces / 240 ml) coconut milk, such as Aroy-D

1 teaspoon cornstarch

1 cup (200 g) sugar

½ teaspoon kosher salt

When I was around twelve or thirteen, entering my hormonal teenage years, my mom would tell me to drink this in order to feel "mát" or "cool." It's believed that grass jelly, made from a plant in the mint family called *Mesona chinensis*, can help reduce heat and inflammation in the body, aiding in matters of the stomach. Though grass jelly comes in a shiny black variety, we also add a firmer white version for added texture. Some people make this dish with only milk and sugar, but we add coconut milk for flavor. There are also basil seeds, which are similar in texture and nutrition to the larger chia seeds. The dish can be served with crushed or cubed ice and can also be stored for 2 to 3 days in an airtight container in the refrigerator (but don't add the coconut milk sauce until it's ready to be served).

Vietnamese Grass Jelly Dessert
Sương Sa Hạt Lựu
Serves 6 to 8

Method

Make the grass jellies: In a 2-quart (2-L) saucepan, mix the white grass jelly powder and sugar. Add 4½ cups (1 L) water and stir until the powder and sugar have dissolved. Set aside and let rest for 30 minutes. Cook over medium heat for 5 minutes, stirring continuously until the white grass jelly mixture thickens. Pour into a 9 by 5-inch (23 by 13-cm) loaf pan, let cool, then cover with plastic wrap and refrigerate for 3 to 4 hours or overnight, until jellied. Cut the jelly into dice-size cubes or any shape of your choosing. Meanwhile, use the same process with the black jelly powder.

Make the coconut milk sauce: In a 2-quart (2-L) saucepan over high heat, bring the coconut milk, condensed milk, and milk to a boil, stirring to combine. Turn off the heat and let the sauce cool.

Make the garnish: Add the dried basil seeds to 1 cup (240 ml) warm water and let soak for 15 minutes, or until the basil seeds are coated with a translucent white film and have doubled in size. Drain out excess water.

Assemble and serve: Layer the white and black grass jelly cubes into individual glasses or bowls, pour on the coconut milk sauce, and then top with the basil seeds and cubed or shaved ice.

Ingredients

FOR THE GRASS JELLIES:
½ cup (50 g) white grass jelly powder, such as Telephồne

½ cup (100 g) sugar

½ cup (50 g) black grass jelly powder, such as Suong Sao

FOR THE COCONUT MILK SAUCE:
1 (14-ounce/400-ml) can coconut milk, such as Aroy-D

½ cup (120 ml) sweetened condensed milk, such as Longevity

1½ cups (360 ml) milk

FOR ASSEMBLY AND SERVING:
3 teaspoons basil seeds

Shaved or cubed ice

Baked Honeycomb Cake
Bánh Bò Nướng

Makes two 9-inch (23-cm) round cakes

While most popular Vietnamese desserts fall into the chè (or dessert "soup" category), bánh bò nướng is a baked pandan-flavored dessert that is widely loved for its chewy, spongy texture. Visually, it's hard to ignore: The pandan gives it a bright green hue, while the tapioca flour creates a gorgeous honeycomb pattern. This is also an important dessert to Yen and her family. For one, it's the best dessert that Yen's mom makes–according to her church, anyway. And when my mother-in-law was bravely battling cancer, making this cake was one of the only things that could get her out of bed. Yen and her mom spent quality time together around the oven, and now it's come to symbolize family. This recipe is simple and foolproof. We whisk by hand, but you're welcome to use a stand mixer if you have one. Note that because of the spongy texture, the cake should be stored for 1 to 2 days at most or else it will harden. It's best served warm, so if reheating, just pop it in the microwave for 15 seconds.

Ingredients

Butter, for greasing the pan

1 (14-ounce/400-ml) can coconut milk, such as Aroy-D

2 cups (380 g) palm sugar (or brown sugar if you cannot find palm sugar)

1½ tablespoons green pandan extract, such as Butterfly

8 large eggs, at room temperature

3 cups (400 g) tapioca flour or starch, such as Erawan

2 packets French cake baking powder, such as Alsa

> **BAKING POWDER**
> We highly recommend using French baking powder because it will help the cakes rise properly.

Method

Preheat the oven to 400°F (205°C) and grease two 9-inch (23-cm) round cake pans.

In a 2-quart (2-L) saucepan over low heat, add the coconut milk and sugar. Stir for 2 minutes, or until the sugar dissolves, then turn off the heat, stir in the pandan extract, and set aside to cool to room temperature, about 20 minutes.

In a large bowl, lightly whisk the eggs. Add the cooled coconut milk and sugar mixture to the whisked eggs along with the tapioca flour and baking powder. Whisk for 3 to 4 minutes. Scrape down the sides of the bowl and mix again for another 1 to 2 minutes, until all the tapioca flour is incorporated and the batter is silky smooth.

Pour the batter into the greased cake pans. Lower the oven temperature to 350°F (175°C) and bake the cakes for 40 to 45 minutes, until golden brown.

Let the cakes cool for 10 minutes in the pan, then unmold and slice to serve.

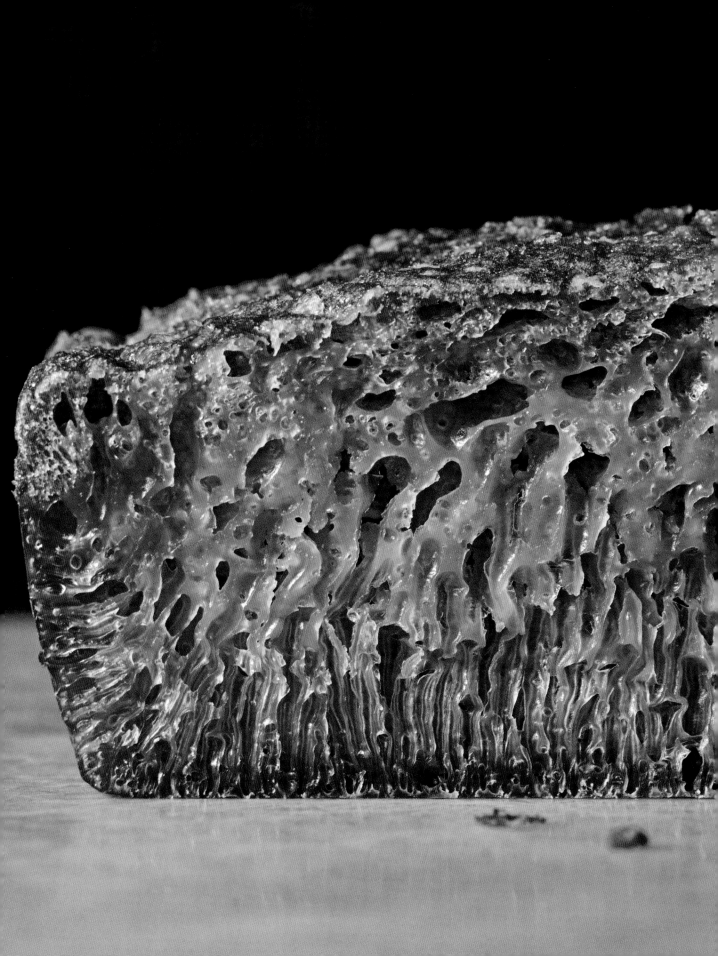

Making bánh chuối hấp is the Vietnamese answer to baking banana bread to use up leftover, overripe bananas, but instead of baking, we steam. This was one of Yen's favorite desserts growing up, and it's a quick and easy recipe she still makes today. You can keep the cake refrigerated in an airtight container for 3 to 4 days. Serve it warm or at room temperature.

Steamed Banana Cake
Bánh Chuối Hấp

Serves 6 to 8

Method

Make the banana cake: In a large bowl, mix the sugar and salt, then add the bananas and, keeping the slices intact, gently mix to coat evenly. Set aside for 15 minutes. Once the coated banana slices have rested, add the tapioca and rice flours and toss gently to combine. Add ¼ cup (60 ml) water into the mixture and gently mix until the water is fully incorporated. Spread the mixture evenly onto a lightly greased 6-inch (15-cm) cake pan.

In a steamer, let the cake steam for 15 to 20 minutes, or until the texture is more akin to a sticky Jell-O. The cake will turn from white to a more translucent color.

Make the coconut milk sauce: In a 2-quart (2-L) saucepan over high heat, bring the coconut milk to a boil. Meanwhile, in a small bowl stir together 3 tablespoons water and the cornstarch. Once the coconut milk is boiling, stir in the cornstarch slurry, sugar, and salt until combined.

Assemble and serve: Let the cake cool for 30 minutes, then cut into squares and serve drizzled with the coconut milk sauce. Garnish with the sesame seeds and crushed peanuts.

Ingredients

FOR THE BANANA CAKE:
1½ tablespoons sugar

½ teaspoon kosher salt

2¼ cups (350 g) peeled and thinly sliced bananas

½ cup (60 g) tapioca flour or starch, such as Erawan

¼ cup (30 g) rice flour

FOR THE COCONUT MILK SAUCE:
1 cup (240 ml) coconut milk, such as Aroy-D

1 teaspoon cornstarch

2 tablespoons sugar

½ teaspoon kosher salt

FOR SERVING:
3½ tablespoons (20 g) toasted sesame seeds

2 tablespoons crushed peanuts

Pandan Sticky Rice
Xôi Lá Dứa

Serves 4 to 6

This is something Vietnamese families make for Lunar New Year, or Tết, and this is my mom's signature recipe. The vibrant green of the pandan sticky rice represents money, so my family says, "Eat more so you can make more money this year!" This is our son Clinton's favorite Vietnamese dessert, and both of our moms make it for him. Sometimes he'll have nothing but pandan sticky rice for dinner. Store-bought pandan extract may be used, but for this dessert, we prefer making it with fresh or frozen pandan leaves because of the incredibly sweet aroma generated by steaming the rice in the homemade pandan extract. Pandan sticky rice can be kept for 1 to 2 days in the refrigerator; bring up to room temperature or warm before serving.

Ingredients

FOR THE PANDAN EXTRACT:
20 to 25 fresh or frozen pandan leaves

FOR THE RICE:
1 (14-ounce/400-ml) can coconut milk, such as Aroy-D

1 cup (200 to 220 g) sweet rice, such as Mei Gui Hua

2 drops green liquid food coloring

1 teaspoon kosher salt

2 to 3 teaspoons sugar

FOR SERVING:
Meat of 1 large (35 to 70 ounces / 1 to 2 kg) fresh coconut, grated

1 pinch sugar

½ cup (65 g) roasted peanuts, crushed (optional)

¼ cup (40 g) toasted sesame seeds (optional)

Method

Make the pandan extract: Wash the pandan leaves and slice them into small pieces, roughly ½ to 1 inch (1.3 to 2.5 cm). Add the sliced pandan to a blender with 1 cup (240 ml) cold water. Purée on high, then use a fine-mesh sieve or cheesecloth to filter the purée to remove any solids from the juice.

Prepare the rice: In a bowl, mix the pandan extract with the canned coconut milk and 4½ cups (1 L) cold water. Mix in the sweet rice, green food coloring, and salt, cover with plastic wrap, and let sit overnight at room temperature.

The next day, strain the sweet rice from the pandan extract mixture and allow the rice to dry completely, about 2 to 3 hours. Spread the cool sweet rice in an even layer in a 9 by 3–inch (23 by 8–cm) round, high-sided cake pan. Pour 4¼ cups (980 ml) water into the bottom of a 3-quart (2.8-L) steamer and place the cake pan in the steamer. Steam over high heat for 30 minutes, until the rice mixture is sticky but not too soft. Once the sweet rice has finished steaming, mix in the sugar to taste.

Assemble and serve: Scoop the rice into bowls or onto plates and top each portion with the coconut, sugar, and, if desired, peanuts and sesame seeds. Serve warm or at room temperature.

Pandan offers comparable flavors and aromas to vanilla and can be used in the form of either fresh syrup or a concentrated extract. Pandan waffles were a childhood favorite for both me and Yen. My family sold them at our old bakery, Paris Sandwich, while Yen grew up thinking they were a totally normal American breakfast food. But they're really a wonderful marriage of two worlds: American and Vietnamese. Today, we make my mom's recipe for our kids all the time. Enjoy the waffles with our coconut whipped cream, a drizzle of sweetened condensed milk, or just some peanut butter spread on top.

Pandan Waffles
Bánh Kẹp Lá Dứa

Makes 8 to 10 waffles
(serves 4 to 6)

Method

Make the pandan extract: Wash the pandan leaves and slice them into small pieces, roughly ½ to 1 inch (1.3 to 2.5 cm). Add the sliced pandan to a blender with 1 cup (240 ml) cold water. Purée on high, then use a fine-mesh sieve or cheesecloth to filter the purée to remove any solids from the juice.

Make the coconut whipped cream (optional): Make sure the coconut milk is well chilled prior to making the whipped cream so that it whips up and holds air. Using an immersion blender or handheld electric mixer with a whisk attachment, whip the chilled coconut milk for 2 minutes on a medium setting, then 2 minutes on high. (Or, add the chilled coconut milk to a whipped cream dispenser, if you own one, and activate it using a whipped cream charger.)

Make the waffles: In a large bowl, crack the eggs. Add the tapioca flour, rice flour, all-purpose flour, sugar, baking powder, salt, and coconut milk to the bowl, and then whisk until combined. Add the pandan extract and whisk until a silky, smooth texture is achieved.

Preheat and coat a waffle iron with nonstick cooking spray. Pour the batter into the iron and cook the waffle according to the manufacturer's instructions. Repeat until you've used up all the batter.

Serve the hot waffles topped with a drizzle of condensed milk and the coconut whipped cream, if using.

Ingredients

FOR THE PANDAN EXTRACT:
10 fresh or frozen pandan leaves (about 1⅓ ounces / 45 g), or 2 tablespoons artificial pandan extract

FOR THE COCONUT WHIPPED CREAM (OPTIONAL):
¾ (14-ounce/400-ml) can coconut milk, such as Aroy-D, chilled for at least 3 hours

FOR THE WAFFLES:
3 large eggs

2 cups (270 g) tapioca flour or starch, such as Erawan

1 cup (160 g) rice flour, such as Erawan

½ cup (65 g) all-purpose flour

¾ cup (150 g) sugar

2¼ teaspoons baking powder

¼ teaspoon kosher salt

1 (14-ounce/400-ml) can coconut milk, such as Aroy-D

Nonstick cooking spray or 1 tablespoon vegetable oil

Sweetened condensed milk, such as Longevity, for serving

Dad's Hangover Cure

Serves 3 to 4

Drinking has always been a part of our culture, and growing up, my family hosted a lot of parties. My dad would always serve fruit and tea to help folks sober up and indicate that it was time to call it a night. At our restaurant Monsieur Vo, we carry on this tradition by combining tropical fruits like guava and mangosteen with green tea on one refreshing plate. A few drops of coriander seed oil (we love the one from Au Natural Organics) and a sprinkle of chile salt help accentuate the natural sweetness of the fruit.

Ingredients

1 guava, skinned and cut into 1½-inch (4-cm) cubes

1 dragon fruit, skinned and cut in 1½-inch (4-cm) cubes

6 mangosteens, peeled

1 Asian pear, skinned, cored, and cut in 2-inch (5-cm) cubes

1 cup (240 ml) jasmine green tea, brewed from 1 tea bag and cooled

5 drops coriander seed oil

Chile Salt for Fruit (page 64)

6 fresh mint leaves

Method

Arrange the cut fruit on a large plate. Pour the cooled tea on top of the fruit and use a dropper to add the coriander oil drops into the mixture. Top with a sprinkle of chile salt and the mint leaves. Serve immediately.

Vietnam is world-renowned for its coffee culture, which originated during the period of French colonization. While the French brought coffee (among other things) to Vietnam, the Vietnamese people have put their own distinct spin on it by using a slow-drip stainless-steel filter, called a phin, and blending the coffee with condensed milk. Cà phê sữa means "milk coffee," whereas Cà phê sữa dá is "iced milk coffee." In the context of Vietnamese coffee, "sữa" almost always means condensed milk, so if you're ordering coffee in Vietnam and want fresh milk, go for sữa tươi.

At Madame Vo, we use a traditional Vietnamese phin filter; however, in a pinch, you can use a regular coffee maker set to the boldest setting possible. Phin filters can be purchased online at any Vietnamese coffee roaster, or even on Amazon. Our American twist is using Café du Monde, a New Orleans–based coffee that's roasted with chicory, which offers a warm, caramel-like aroma.

Note: Café du Monde is not the type of coffee consumed in Vietnam; it has been adopted by Vietnamese Americans who sought out a local, bold, dark coffee to use. That's not to say we don't also love trying specialty coffee grown in Vietnam, such as those made by roasters like Nam Coffee.

. DRINKS .

Vietnamese Milk Coffee
Cà Phê Sữa Đá

Makes 1 drink

Method

Spoon your ground coffee into the chamber of the phin filter, then place the filter press on top. Don't press down too hard. Pour ½ cup (120 ml) boiling water into the press. Let it drip into a heat-safe cup for roughly 5 minutes, or until all the liquid has dripped into the cup. Add the condensed milk to an 8-ounce (240-ml) cup. Pour the coffee directly into the condensed milk and stir to combine.

For the iced version, let the coffee cool to room temperature then pour into a 10-ounce (300-ml) glass. Add ice and fill to the top. Serve the coffee with a long spoon for stirring.

Ingredients

2 tablespoons ground Café du Monde coffee (see Note)

1½ tablespoons condensed milk

Vietnamese Espresso Martini

Makes 1 cocktail

Espresso martinis have been one of the biggest cocktail drink trends of recent years, and given our love of coffee, it's a drink that we have been wanting to put our own spin on. My co-author, Dan Q. Dao, a former bartender, collaborated with us to create a 100-percent Vietnamese cocktail made with a stunning Vietnamese gin, from the pioneering Hanoi-based Sông Cái Distillery, and Vietnamese coffee, from a roaster like Nam Coffee, brewed the traditional way in a stainless steel phin filter. The best coffee to use for this would be dark robusta bean.

Ingredients

FOR THE COFFEE:
2 tablespoons ground Vietnamese robusta coffee, such as Nam Coffee Da Lat

FOR THE COCKTAIL:
½ ounce (15 ml) coffee liqueur, such as Mr. Black

2 ounces (60 ml) Sông Cái Floral Gin

½ ounce (15 ml) sweetened condensed milk

3 coffee beans, for garnish

Method

Brew the coffee: Spoon ground coffee into the chamber of the phin filter, then place the filter press on top. Don't press down too hard. Pour ½ cup (120 ml) of boiling water into the press. Let it drip into a heat-safe cup for roughly 5 minutes, or until all the liquid is in the cup. Let cool to room temperature.

Make the cocktail: Combine the coffee, coffee liqueur, gin, and condensed milk in a shaker tin, add 6 to 8 cubes of ice, and shake vigorously for 10 to 15 seconds, or until the tin frosts over. Use a hawthorne strainer to strain the drink into a chilled martini glass and garnish with the coffee beans.

Avocado Smoothie
Sinh Tố Bơ

Makes one 8-ounce
(240-ml) smoothie

In Vietnam, avocados are used not only for savory dishes but also for desserts. Growing up, Yen's favorite afternoon snack was simply a ripe avocado sliced open, with condensed milk drizzled on top. This combination is also popular in smoothie form, blending with half-and-half and ice for a thick, frozen treat. For a dairy-free version, you may use vegan condensed milk (available online) and a barista blend of oat milk in lieu of half-and-half.

Ingredients

½ ripe avocado, peeled and pitted

¼ cup (60 ml) sweetened condensed milk, such as Longevity

3 ounces (90 ml) half-and-half

1 cup (220 g) ice

Method

Add the avocado, condensed milk, half-and-half, and ice to a blender. Blend on high setting for 3 to 4 minutes, until smooth. Pour into a tall glass and serve cold.

Vietnam, specifically the Mekong Delta region, is famous for coconuts. When Madame Vo first opened, we sold so many whole fresh coconuts in the restaurant, it was a coconut craze. So, we decided to take things one step further and turn coconut into a smoothie. For a dairy-free version, you may use vegan condensed milk (available online) and a barista blend of oat milk in lieu of half-and-half.

Coconut Smoothie
Sinh Tố Dừa

Makes three 8-ounce (240-ml) smoothies

Method

Add the coconut meat, condensed milk, half-and-half, and ice to a blender. Blend on high setting for 3 to 4 minutes, until smooth. Divide among three tall glasses and serve cold.

Ingredients

1 fresh coconut, meat scraped out using a coconut opener tool (available online) or using a butcher knife to cut the coconut in half and a spoon to scrape out the meat

½ cup (120 ml) sweetened condensed milk, such as Longevity

¼ cup (60 ml) half-and-half

3 cups (720 g) ice

Durian is the king of all Southeast Asian fruits. It famously has a distinct, pungent smell that has gotten it banned from airplanes, hotels, and other public places. When we visited Vietnam when I was little, I remember buying a bunch of durian from a street vendor. We got scolded by our hotel, which was the funniest thing. Honestly, I hated durian as a kid and only learned to love it as I grew older. For beginners, a smoothie–with condensed milk and half-and-half–takes a little bit of the edge off. In a smoothie, the fruit has a wonderful thick and creamy texture that resembles ice cream.

Durian Smoothie
Sinh Tố Sầu Riêng

Makes one 12-ounce (360-ml) smoothie

Method

Add the durian meat, condensed milk, half-and-half, and ice to a blender. Blend on high setting for 3 to 4 minutes, until smooth.

Pour it into a tall glass and serve cold. Garnish with whipped cream, if desired, and serve cold.

Ingredients

7 ounces (200 g) fresh or frozen seedless durian meat

¼ cup (60 ml) sweetened condensed milk

6 tablespoons (90 ml) half-and-half

1 cup (220 g) ice

Dollop whipped cream (optional)

First Kiss

Makes 1 drink

This cocktail puts the spotlight on chrysanthemum, a bright yellow flower often found in bouquets and decorations for the Lunar New Year, or Tết. Also enjoyed in dishes like soup and drinks like tea, it lends a fragrant, herbaceous, and green taste. Here, it's infused in vodka and then shaken up with fresh lemon, an Italian bergamot orange liqueur, and a rose-flavored syrup for an extra floral note. Purchase dried chrysanthemum online or in an Asian supermarket.

Ingredients

FOR THE CHRYSANTHEMUM-INFUSED VODKA:

1 cup (240 ml) vodka

¾ cup (43 g) food-grade dried chrysanthemum

FOR THE COCKTAIL:

2 ounces (60 ml) chrysanthemum-infused vodka (see above)

¾ ounce (22 ml) fresh lemon juice

½ ounce (15 ml) Italicus Rosolio Bergamot Liqueur

½ ounce (15 ml) rose simple syrup, such as Monin Premium Rose Flavoring

Food-grade dried chrysanthemum, for garnish (optional)

Method

Infuse the vodka: Pour the vodka into a jar and add the chrysanthemum to infuse. Let the infusion sit for 2 hours 45 minutes, then strain through a fine-mesh strainer and return to the jar. Infused spirits are best enjoyed within four months when stored in a cool, dry place.

Make the cocktail: In a mixing glass, combine the chrysanthemum-infused vodka, lemon juice, bergamot liqueur, and rose syrup. Top off with ice and stir for 10 to 15 seconds, or until thoroughly chilled.

Strain into a rocks glass filled with ice. Garnish with a sprinkling of the dried flowers, if you like, and serve.

Le Secret d'Amour

Makes 1 drink

This is our take on a rum cocktail with a distinctly Southeast Asian flair, thanks to the addition of passion fruit purée, which you can purchase at the grocery store. Though the strong, tart flavor of passion fruit could be overpowering in a drink, we temper it with dashes of five-spice bitters, which offers strong notes of warm pepper and anise.

Ingredients

2 ounces (60 ml) white rum, such as Bacardí

½ ounce (15 ml) passion fruit purée

Splash Aperol

2 dashes five-spice bitters, such as Shanghai Shirley

Star anise (optional)

Method

In a mixing glass, combine the white rum, passion fruit purée, Aperol, and five-spice bitters. Top with ice and stir for 10 to 15 seconds, or until thoroughly chilled.

Strain into a rocks glass filled with ice. Garnish with some star anise, if you like, and serve.

First Kiss (left) and
Le Secret d'Amour (right)

Miss Saigon

Makes 1 drink

Plum is widely used in candies and drinks throughout Asia, and we wanted to create a cocktail that features traditional plum wine as the main ingredient. Plum wine is a great aperitif on its own, but pairs well with peach, which brightens up the concentrated sweetness of plum. We added vodka to give it a kick, with fresh mint and lime juice to freshen everything up.

Ingredients

Kosher salt (optional)

1 ounce (30 ml) vodka, such as Ketel One

1 ounce (30 ml) plum wine, such as Choya

¾ ounce (22 ml) peach liqueur, such as De Kuyper

¾ ounce (22 ml) lime simple syrup

3 fresh mint leaves

Method

Rim a coupe glass with kosher salt, if desired.

In a cocktail shaker, combine the vodka, plum wine, peach liqueur, lime syrup, and mint leaves. Fill with ice and shake for 10 to 15 seconds, until thoroughly chilled and the metal of the shaker tin frosts over.

Double strain into the rimmed coupe glass.

Madame Sour

Makes 1 drink

Like Vietnamese food, our take on the traditional sour is complex and aromatic. You get botanical notes from the gin, herbaceous flavors from the basil, and fruity and flowery accents from the lychee.

Ingredients

2 ounces (60 ml) Song Cai Viet Nam Dry gin

½ ounce (15 ml) fresh lemon juice

½ ounce (15 ml) lychee simple syrup, such as Tea Zone

3 fresh basil leaves, plus 1 for garnish

Lime zest (optional)

Method

In a cocktail shaker, combine the gin, lemon juice, lychee syrup, and basil leaves. Top with ice and shake until thoroughly chilled.

Double strain into a coupe glass, garnish with a basil leaf and lime zest, if using, and serve.

Madame Sour

Created by Yen's brother Khanh, our beverage director, this drink riffs on a classic cocktail called the Paper Plane, made with bourbon, amaro nonino, Aperol, and lemon juice. In this revision, we swap the bourbon for añejo tequila, the amaro nonino for amaro Montenegro, and the Aperol for Pimms No. 1, to yield a fruity, citrusy profile.

Paper Lantern

Makes 1 drink

Method

In a cocktail shaker, combine the añejo tequila, Pimms No. 1, Amaro Montenegro, lemon juice, and simple syrup. Top with several cubes of ice and shake vigorously for 10 to 15 seconds, or until the outside of the tin frosts over.

Double strain into a chilled coupe glass. Garnish with an orange or lime wheel.

Ingredients

¾ ounce (22 ml) añejo tequila

¾ ounce (22 ml) Pimms No. 1

¾ ounce (22 ml) Amaro Montenegro

¾ ounce (22 ml) fresh lemon juice

½ ounce (15 ml) simple syrup

Orange or lime wheel

THE MADAME VO
Mini-Guide to NYC

As diehard New Yorkers, we feel lucky to be living in the greatest city for food. From the mom-and-pop Asian spots I grew up with in Queens to our treat-yourself date spots, Yen and I have a long list of restaurants and other businesses where we consider ourselves regulars and fans. For your next NYC food adventure, here is just a small selection of our favorite places to eat and buy groceries.

WHERE TO EAT (NON-VIETNAMESE FOOD)

Queens High Pearl (Queens)
This is our favorite old-school Chinese restaurant in New York City that's been around forever. Located in Elmhurst, they serve an extensive menu of mostly Cantonese and seafood dishes, including standouts like the walnut shrimp, Peking pork chop, and beef chow fun that comes with peppers and a savory black bean gravy.

Jeong Yook (Queens)
While we eat Vietnamese barbecue at home, we love to go out for Korean BBQ as a family. Jeong Yook in Flushing's Chinatown area is our kids' favorite spot, and they always ask to go there. We love that the restaurant provides lots of banchan (the complimentary dishes, like pickled veggies and kimchi, that come with KBBQ) and the gochujang chili sauce that comes with the meat. Go for the galbi (marinated beef short rib) and you won't be disappointed.

Asian Jewels Dim Sum (Queens)
Also in Flushing, Asian Jewels is hands down one of the best Hong Kong–style dim sum restaurants in the city. They just have that classic Chinatown flavor and vibe that I knew growing up. Our go-to dim sum order is beef rice rolls, fried doughnut rice rolls, and mochi balls with peanut paste.

Jaew Hon (Queens)
Thai hot pot is a mind-blowing experience of spice and flavor. In Elmhurst, which is known for its Thai restaurants, seek out Jaew Hon, a northern Thai, or Isan, specialist that offers an incredibly good-value, all-you-can-eat buffet. Hot pot is super customizable: Choose from soup bases like classic tom yum or tom zap, a dark spicy soup with lime juice, fish sauce, and rice powder. The secret to hot pot is the sauces: Jaew Hon has different ones designed for meat, seafood, or both.

Double Chicken Please (Manhattan)
When we need a drink, we love hopping over to Double Chicken Please on the Lower East Side. We're big fans of bartender GN Chan's experimental cocktails, especially the ones that use Asian flavors—including many of the ones found in this book, from lemongrass to tea. In addition, they also have fun bar snacks like a salted egg yolk chicken sandwich and a hojicha pudding.

Rubirosa (Manhattan)
A New York City restaurant list isn't complete without pizza. Our top slice is the Staten Island-style, thin crust, red-sauced one from Nolita's iconic Rubirosa. Simple and perfect.

Mister Softee ice cream, a staple growing up in NYC

Lady Wong (Manhattan)
There historically have not been many Southeast Asian bakeries in NYC. Most of the ones in Chinatown are Chinese or Japanese. A hop, skip, and a jump away from Madame Vo in the East Village, Lady Wong offers pastries, rice-based desserts, and other sweet snacks from Malaysia, Indonesia, Thailand, Vietnam, and beyond. Many of the flavors they use are present in this book, like pandan and coconut. Their pandan nian gao is similar to our Baked Honeycomb Cake (page 214), and they also offer bánh da lợn, a Vietnamese treat with tapioca flour, rice flour, and mung beans.

Clinton Street Baking Company (Manhattan)
This Lower East Side establishment is our weekend brunch standby, offering standards like eggs Benedict and chicken and waffles. Though they're best-known for their pancakes, specifically the blueberry pancakes, we also stop by sometimes just for the signature black-and-white layer cake, which is one of our favorite desserts in NYC.

Au Cheval (Manhattan)
Last, but not least, is our ultimate burger restaurant. Burgers are my favorite everyday American food, and Au Cheval's burgers are considered by many to be the best in town. Sometimes two prime beef patties, melted American cheese, and pickles is all you need.

WHERE TO BUY VIETNAMESE GROCERIES

Tan Tin Hung (Manhattan)
This is the essential, if not only, major Vietnamese grocery in New York City these days. Located on Bowery in Manhattan's Chinatown, they've got all the herbs, canned goods, and dried goods you'll need for this book.

If you're in NYC and trying your hand at the recipes in this book, you'll definitely want to stop by.

US Supermarket (Queens)
Located in Elmhurst, this Asian supermarket is our local spot for groceries when we're in Queens. Like Tan Tin Hung, they carry a large variety of tough-to-find Asian herbs like Vietnamese coriander and banana leaf. They also have a great meat selection, and we usually stop here to pick up our bones to make stock for phở (pages 123, 129, and 132).

THE MADAME VO
Mini-Guide to Saigon

We are always looking back to our parents' homeland in Vietnam, and of course the vibrant, dynamic, and rapidly modernizing city of Saigon, now called Ho Chi Minh City, which has inspired the heart of our cooking and our bold flavors. Though it's been several years since we've been back to Vietnam—it's tough to find the time while running two restaurants and raising two kids—we can't wait to make it back. Here, we're sharing our guide to modern Vietnamese places to stay, eat, and drink, and a couple of places you have to see while you're there.

WHERE TO STAY

Reverie
Arguably one of the swankiest hotels in Southeast Asia, the 286-room, Italian-inspired Reverie stuns on arrival with three thousand tons of marble—much of which is seen when you walk into the lobby. Set in Saigon's third-tallest building, the hotel has an open-air rooftop deck, four restaurants, and a fleet of luxury cars to pick you up from the airport.

Hotel Continental Saigon
Built in 1880 by French construction supply firm Pierre Cazeau, this is the oldest still-standing hotel in Saigon. With spacious rooms and a prime location on Dong Khoi Street, it remains an iconic property worth checking out.

Hôtel Des Arts Saigon
For a boutique option, this modern hotel offers sweeping skyline views of the cityscape. It's ideal for couples who want to relax, grab a drink at the swim-up bar, or check out the curated art selection.

WHERE TO EAT AND DRINK

Anan
The creation of Chef Peter Cuong Franklin, Anan brought global recognition to Vietnamese food in 2013 when it became the first restaurant in Vietnam to make it onto the World's Best Restaurants list, and it has appeared on the list every year since. In 2023, it also became the only Michelin-starred restaurant in Saigon. Featuring a modern take on Vietnamese cuisine, which Chef Franklin dubs "New Vietnamese," or Cuisine Moi, the menu has included standout dishes like bánh xèo tacos and bone marrow phở.

Esta
In recent years, Western-influenced wood-fired cooking has become popular in modern Saigon restaurants. Led by Chef Francis Thuan, who was formerly an engineer by trade, Esta spotlights ingredients sourced locally from his home region in the Central Highlands, utilized in modern gastronomic interpretations.

Hum Vegetarian
Although Vietnamese dishes typically contain meat, many people influenced by Buddhist traditions choose to eat vegetarian, or ăn chay, regularly, or at least on the first day of the month in the lunar calendar. Hum reimagines classic Vietnamese foods, like thịt kho, or caramelized braised pork, in vegetarian form—made with tofu.

Bánh Mì Huỳnh Hoa
Opened in 1989, Bánh mì Huỳnh Hoa is one of the most iconic sandwich stalls in the city, serving sandwiches with fillings both hot, like grilled pork, and cold, like Vietnamese cold cuts and head cheese.

RIGHT: Bến Thành Market, Saigon

Nhớ Tuyết

Vietnamese gastropub-style dining and drinking, or ăn nhậu, is a bedrock of Vietnamese culture. One of the OG destinations for seafood cooked to order, including snails, giant prawns, crab, and lobster, Nhớ Tuyết is a great place for friends and family to gather over fresh seafood served with plenty of beer.

Hue Café Roastery

Vietnam is the world's second-largest exporter of coffee, much of it robusta, which is the darker, more chocolatey of the two common types of coffee bean that are grown commercially (the other is arabica, which is considered to be lighter and fruitier). Hue Café is a must-visit destination for traditional Vietnamese coffee such as cà phê đá, crafted with local Vietnamese beans and a bold flavor profile. Its signature drink is a whipped and salted milk coffee that originated in the former imperial city of Huế.

The Workshop

Beyond robusta, Vietnam also produces a small amount of specialty arabica coffee in the highland region. The Workshop spotlights specialty beans from the country, and introduces modern third-wave coffee culture to Saigon, with thoughtful versions of pour-overs and espresso drinks.

Rabbit Hole

While Vietnam's cocktail culture is still developing, Rabbit Hole was one of the first to bring attention to the scene. The Art Deco–style speakeasy channels the cocktail culture of New York but integrates local flavors and ingredients into spirited form.

WHAT TO SEE

Bưu Điện (Post Office)

There's no shortage of French colonial architecture in Saigon, but the bưu điện, or post office, is one of the best structures that remains standing—and functioning as a real post office—today.

Fine Arts Museum

Set in another former French colonial building, Saigon's fine arts museum is small but worth a visit, showcasing oil paintings, watercolor on silk, and sculptures from the pre-war era through today.

Bến Thành Market

Perhaps the most famous market in all of Vietnam, Bến Thành is a bustling maze of vendors hawking everything from souvenirs to local silk clothing. Within the chaos of it all, there's also a sizable food market with twenty-some vendors serving an array of noodle soups, street food, and Vietnamese desserts. At sunset, the day market closes and an outdoor night market opens, offering a more relaxed shopping experience.

THANK YOU!

Jimmy Ly

Writing my own cookbook was one of my biggest lifetime aspirations as a chef. And ever since we opened Madame Vo, we have dreamed of sharing our own recipes with the community. We are so thankful for the opportunity given to us after all the hardships and doubt we endured throughout the pandemic.

To Yen Vo: My wife and my biggest cheerleader. You have always supported me in all my endeavors—even quitting your job and following me down this path of opening my own restaurant. Your light always shined the brightest during our darkest times. Thank you for pushing me to be the best version of myself. I love you so much.

To my parents: Mom and Dad, you have taught me everything I know about Vietnamese cooking and food. Thank you for all the sacrifices you made and the dedication you showed, just for us to have a better life. I wouldn't be where I am today without your guidance.

To my Madame Vo and Monsieur Vo family—all past, present, and future staff: You guys are a huge part of our restaurants, and it wouldn't be possible if it weren't for your daily grind and the devotion you have shown to our patrons. Creating a sense of dining in our home was the philosophy we have always stood by. Thank you, team.

To Dan Q. Dao, our writer: We'll never forget the first time we met at Madame Vo. It was like we had already known each other. You loved the food, and you loved us. Thank you for always supporting us from the very beginning and becoming our little brother. It's an honor for you to be the writer of our first cookbook. Thank you for putting all my thoughts into a cohesive narrative. I know it wasn't easy.

To Sarah Jessica Parker: Thank you for sharing your voice and telling people how good our food is. We forever consider you our fairy godmother. It's still surreal to us. You were the one person that believed in us when nobody did. Thank you for giving us the platform we have today. On behalf of my family and team, we are forever grateful.

To Laura Dozier: For being not only our editor in chief but also our biggest supporter and a patron of our restaurants. We couldn't be more grateful to have worked with you and learned so much in this process. Thank you for your endless energy and patience in making this book as user-friendly, coherent, and perfect as possible. You made our dream come true.

To our designer, Diane Shaw: Thank you for your vision and direction in making this book a visually cohesive work of art—you rock.

To the entire team at Abrams Books: From copy editors to publicity, thank you for believing in the brand and the book—it was just a pleasure.

To Ian Kleinert at Paradigm Talent Agency: For being our book agent, we're grateful for you and all that you have done to make this dream a reality. We never thought we could get to this point, but you were that one person that made it happen. Thank you, brother.

To Katelyn Dougherty: Thank you for dealing with all the day-to-day tasks, emails, meetings, and coordination. You were the most patient and beautiful person throughout this entire process. Thank you for always rooting for us.

To our photographer, Andrew Bui; food stylist, Thu Buser; and prop stylist, Charlotte Havelange: It was so important to us to have an all-star, all-Vietnamese team behind this book. Not only are you guys Vietnamese, you're also the most talented and hardworking people we have ever come across. They said it couldn't be done: shooting 75 recipes in five days. But we did it together. That was one for the books and will forever be a memory that we all went through together. The talent, tenacity, and passion were bar none. It was truly an honor to work with you guys. We couldn't be happier with how it came out. Thank you.

To our patrons and supporters: You guys are the reason we do it. If it wasn't for your support, I don't think I could have made this happen. Thank you for always being brutally honest and pushing us to be better. We have met so many amazing customers over the years and built great lasting relationships to this day. You guys are the main reason we love this work so much, and always keep pushing. Thank you everyone for being so awesome.

To the East Village community: Thank you for letting us call the East Village home. This community has always been so good to us.

To Ngan Nguyen: Chi Ngan, our big sister who supported us from the beginning of my Paris Sandwich days. The love of Vietnamese food brought us together. I'll never forgot the day we met: our Bún Bò Huế took you back home when you visited us and struck a conversation. Thank you for always standing in our corner with your love and support from asking us to cater your parties and just being a patron at our restaurant. Over the years you really became our big sister and mentor. Yen and I are ever so grateful for you and your family, and wanted you to know how much we value our relationship. You have been a major contributor to this book and we can't thank you enough.

To Anna Spangler, our recipe tester: It was such a pleasure to work with you through this process. Thank you for your insight and knowledge about food and helping us putting it all on paper. It was a lot of fun.

To all my friends and family: The list goes on and if I had to name everyone, it would take another book. But you know who you are and it takes a village to build this. From the bottom of my heart, we always and forever remember the outpouring of support and love for each and every one of y'all. Life is never easy, but with the right people it truly makes things brighter. So I thank you guys for being a big part of why I do it and keep pushing.

To NYC: The greatest city of all. You made life hard, you made me doubt myself, you broke me, and you made me who I am today. I thank you for shaping me to be who I am today—for teaching me grit and dedication. You have molded me to be better every day.

Yen Vo

To my parents, who always wanted the best for me: You came to America with nothing yet gave me everything and more. No matter how long your days were you always made sure we had a home-cooked meal together every night. These meals created such happy memories for me. Thank you

for your support, guidance, and unconditional love.

To my brother Khanh: Thank you for your love and encouragement. You always sacrificed so your sister could have the best. I love you!

To my babies, Benjamin and Clinton: May you get to live out your dreams.

To my Aunt Hanh: Thank you for pushing me to move to New York. You and Uncle Aaron have guided me since day one here. I am forever thankful for all your love and support.

To our friends that have become family—Kat Nguyen, Steven Chan, Vyky Lam, Lisa Lu, Matt Peng, and Thuy Duong: Thank you.

Dan Q. Dao

Thank you to my family—mom, dad, Auntie Hoa—for instilling within me a sense of pride in being Vietnamese, teaching me so much about Vietnamese food, and inspiring me with all the sacrifices you've made for me to be where I am today.

About Us

Jimmy Ly and Yen Vo

Chef Jimmy Ly and Yen Vo are the husband-wife duo behind the critically acclaimed Vietnamese restaurants Madame Vo and Monsieur Vo, both in New York City's East Village.

Hailing from Queens, New York, Jimmy grew up as the unofficial sous-chef for his immigrant parents. Though he didn't originally plan on becoming a restaurateur, and briefly studied business at New York University, Jimmy eventually decided to drop out and follow in his parents' footsteps to lead the family business at Paris Sandwich, a Vietnamese restaurant in Chinatown. Meanwhile, Yen was born in a refugee camp in Thailand and grew up in Long Beach, Mississippi. She attended university in Houston and moved to New York City to pursue a career in merchandising.

Jimmy and Yen met in 2011 and immediately bonded over a shared love of Vietnamese food. Together, they opened Madame Vo in 2017 to bring homestyle Vietnamese cooking to New York City. In 2018, Jimmy and Yen opened their second restaurant, Madame Vo BBQ, New York City's first-ever Vietnamese barbecue restaurant, which was transformed into Monsieur Vo during the COVID-19 pandemic—a challenging time for the local restaurant industry.

To date, Madame Vo and Monsieur Vo have been featured in the *New York Times*, *The New Yorker*, *Bloomberg*, *Hypebeast*, *Vogue*, and *Saveur*, among others. And Jimmy has appeared in dozens of news and video segments as an on-air expert and educator on Vietnamese food.

In their off time, Jimmy and Yen enjoy cooking, traveling, and spending time with their family, particularly their two young sons, Benjamin and Clinton.

Dan Q. Dao

Dan Q. Dao is a culture writer whose work has appeared in the *New York Times*, *Condé Nast Traveler*, *Vice*, *GQ*, *Food & Wine*, and many more publications. He has also worked with numerous brands and companies like Suntory, Aman Resorts, and Leading Hotels of the World. He got his start in 2015 as an editor covering NYC bars and restaurants at *Time Out New York*, and has since held staff roles at *Saveur* and *Paper*. At the time of writing, Dan is based in Vietnam, but he will one day find his way back to New York, as well as his hometown, Houston. Besides writing, he runs his own food and drink consultancy, District One Studios.

Index

Editor: Laura Dozier
Designer: Diane Shaw
Design Manager: Jenice Kim
Managing Editor: Logan Hill
Production Managers: Larry Pekarek and Kathleen Gaffney

Library of Congress Control Number: 2024933743

ISBN: 978-1-4197-6726-5
eISBN: 978-1-64700-975-5

ABRAMS The Art of Books
195 Broadway, New York, NY 10007
abramsbooks.com